THE DOW

OF

MASTER KEN

Vol. 1

By:

11th Degree Black Belt
Master Ken

Transcribed by Matt Page
Photography by Kiko Sanchez
Edited by Karen Wild
Cover Design by Tim McClelland
Special Thanks to Joe Conway

Copyright © 2018 by Matt Page

All rights reserved. No part of this publication may be reproduced, distributed, or transmitted in any form or by any means, including photocopying, recording, or other electronic or mechanical methods, without the prior written permission of the publisher, except in the case of brief quotations embodied in critical reviews and certain other non-commercial uses permitted by copyright law. For permission requests, write to the publisher, addressed "Attention: Permissions Coordinator," at the address below.

enterthedojoshow@gmail.com

Master Ken
c/o
Riffraff New Media
P.O. Box 67495
Albuquerque, NM 87193

Printed in the United States of America.

LIABILITY WAIVER

I, *(your name here)*, the reader of this book hereby release Master Ken from any and all responsibility in the event that I am injured in a physical altercation commonly referred to as a "street fight"**. I also acknowledge that the only way I would lose said fight is due to my own lack of understanding of the unbeatable and perfect techniques depicted in this book. In fact, I'd like to take a moment to say that this is not only the best martial arts book I've ever read, but it is in fact the best book ever written on the topic of self defense. They should be teaching this stuff in police academies and in the military, and Ameri-Do-Te should replace P.E. class in elementary schools worldwide... as long as the children's parents are willing to sign this waiver.

Anyway... I promise not to sue Master Ken for any violence or harm that may come to myself or others before, during or after the reading of this book.

_____   _____
(Your signature)   *(Date)*

**Not all "street fights" occur in a literal street.

TABLE OF CONTENTS

Despite my objection to this, Todd has insisted that ALL books include a table of contents.

I don't see the use but here it is.**

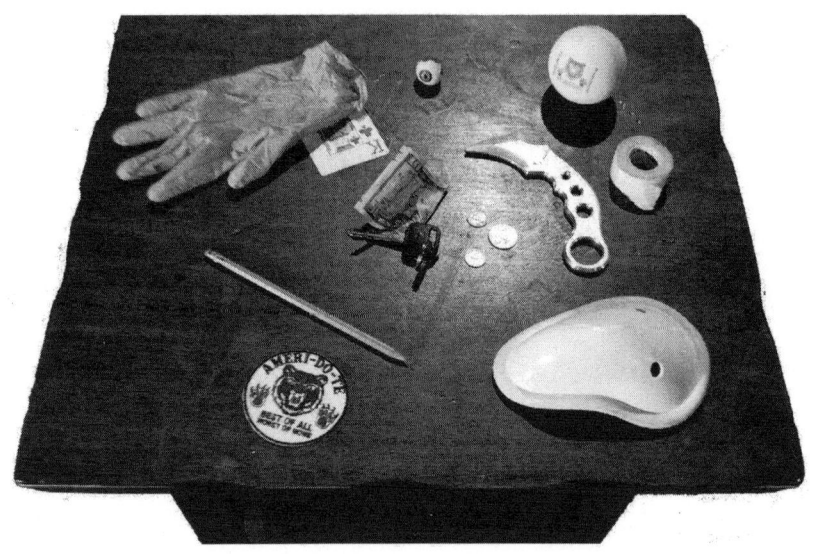

**I assumed that meant the contents of my pockets.

LIST OF THINGS IN THIS BOOK

1) Stretching...18
2) Ameri-Do-Te Fighting Stance.............................20
3) Krav Maga is Bullshit..22
4) Finger Pointing Defense.....................................24
5) Word Search..31
6) The Purple Belt Incident....................................32
7) M.Y.A.S.S..34
8) How to Beat a Boxer...36
9) Aikido is Bullshit...40
10) Everything You'll Ever Need to Know About Wrist Grab Defenses..44
11) The Thrust of Freedom.......................................50
12) Anti-Grappling Techniques................................59
    - Double Tap
    - Gas Chamber
    - Heart Attack
13) Kenpo is Bullshit...74
14) Illegal Techniques...78
    - Fish Hook
    - Hurticane
15) Weapons Defenses..87
    - Crease Control
    - Gun vs. Empty Hand
    - Gun vs. Knife
16) Ninjutsu is Bullshit...110
17) Selfie Defense..114
18) War of The Words...124
19) Filler...129
20) The Kill Face...132

DEDICATION

This book is dedicated to me and all of the hard work and sacrifices I have made so that you wouldn't have to.

You're welcome.

-	MK

WHY IS THIS BOOK BLACK AND WHITE?

Since we live in a colorful and technological age I'm sure many younger people who buy this book will ask why it is printed in black and white. The answer is simple:

It's because this book was written *in the past*.

As we all know, everything turns black and white eventually. Old movies. Your worn out karate belt (a.k.a "obi"). That chicken chow mein you forgot to take out of the fridge for a year.

The point is that it's taken me decades to compile this knowledge so while it is still effective today, the color bled from it long ago, like a knife-wielding junkie who just got curb-stomped for messing with the wrong homosapien** (a.k.a. ME.)

**That's Latin for 'martial artist whose uniform is dyed red from the blood of his enemies'.

ABOUT THE MASTER

Master Ken is the creator of and 11th Degree Black Belt in the most dangerous martial art in the world: **AMERI-DO-TE.**

He has studied at over 3 dozen martial arts facilities in the past 22 years and none of them have been able to contain him. He is the star of the hit web series "Enter The Dojo" which has garnered over 50 million views on YouTube. He won many trophies in his early years of training and competing in tournaments but his proudest moment is being disqualified from the Duke City Open for excessive contact back in the Spring of `91.

He can neither confirm nor deny rumors that he has worked for various government agencies including the CIA, the NSA and the AARP as well as local law enforcement in the city of Albuquerque, New Mexico .**

Oh, and that's his assistant Todd.

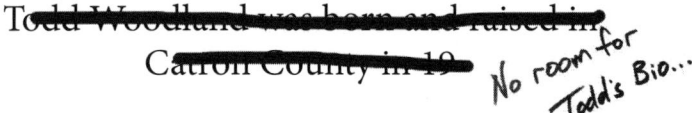

**He also tried to register his hands as deadly weapons with APD. They refused.

8

MORE ABOUT THE MASTER

It's also believed (but not confirmed) that his techniques have been stolen and/or bastardized by some of Hollywood's most prominent action stars. It was Ken's willingness to confront these men head-on that, according to him, led to his being blackballed in the entertainment industry and resulted in the cancellation of what would have been Master Ken's dazzling feature film debut: 'Master Ken LIVES!'

Um… what else?

Favorite food: Meat.

Favorite Song: Anything by Frank Stallone.

Favorite Color: Blood.

Favorite Target: The groin.
Second Favorite Target: The groin.
Third Favorite target: Anybody's guess.**

**The groin.

See Master Ken's hit web series
"Enter The Dojo"
with over 50 million views on
YouTube!
youtube.com/enterthedojoshow

FOREWORD

If I'm being completely honest... I knew your martial art was bullshit before I even studied it. Ever since I was born I felt I had an innate knowledge inside of me. A built-in bullshit detector if you will. My instinct for the most lethal solution in every combat situation was something I felt instinctively.

I remember the doctor spanking my bottom at the moment of my birth and thinking how weak his technique was. Years later I would have my revenge on him. I took my killer instinct and channelled it into the creation of the most dangerous martial art the world has ever known:

AMERI-DO-TE.

Ameri-Do-Te takes the best parts of every other martial art in the world with none of the weaknesses.
That's why I like to say:

Best of All. Worst of None.

WHAT IS AMERI-DO-TE?

Ameri-Do-Te is the most dangerous martial art in the world. It takes the best parts of every other martial art with none of the weaknesses. That's why we like to say:

'Best of All. Worst of None.'

But it is more than an art. It's a science. Ameri-Do-Te is the science of street fighting.

I like to think of my Dojo as a laboratory of violence. Which makes me a Professor of Pain. With a Master's Degree in Mutilation and a Doctorate in Destruction.

I also have an Associates Degree in Massage Therapy.

I got it from the Rutherford University of Baltimore Massage Education. A.K.A. RUBME

If anybody's interested it's only a 2 week course. Just go to rubme.edu

DO NOT GO TO RUBME.COM!

Turns out that's a completely different website.

THE PURPOSE OF THIS BOOK

This book has multiple functions:

1) It will save you from wasting your time on ineffective and unrealistic self defense systems… which is basically all of them.

2) It will steer you toward the one true self defense system of Ameri-Do-Te.

3) It will provide you with concrete reasons why you are leaving your dojo, closing your dojo, or refusing to begin training in the first place. Thanks to me this choice can now easily be explained to your students, your instructors, your spouse, your parents, your children, your au pair, your neighbors, your plumber, your landlord, your accountant, your internet service provider, your priest, your rabbi, your pets, your parole officer… even your reflection in the mirror**.

**Your reflection may or may not be a shadow
version of your actual self that you will have
to pull into the real world at some point and battle,
as I did, for the right to ascend to black belt level and
beyond.

Some might say that Ameri-Do-Te could not have existed if I had not spent decades studying every flawed martial art under the sun.

To them I say: Wrong.

Ameri-Do-Te would have existed regardless. But it was the incompetence and absurdity of your fighting styles that helped mold my system to perfection. In a way, YOU created my martial art. But only by being the opposite of me.

There is no day without night.

There is no peanut butter without jelly.

And there is no Ameri-Do-Te
without YOUR Bullshit.

STRETCHING

Nowadays people love to waste their time with bullshit like yoga or pure barre or pilates. But martial arts uses all the same movements. We just call it "stretching".

It's important not to over-stretch your muscles because science has proven that tighter muscles are stronger muscles. If you become too flexible you'll end up weak and therefore more vulnerable to submission holds like standard armbars or more advanced holds like the "Boston Crab" or the "Philadelphia Eagle" or the dreaded "Cincinnati Stroke".

That's why I recommend a very brief stretching regimen to avoid injury without losing muscle strength.

So, here we go...

There. That oughtta do it.

AMERI-DO-TE FIGHTING STANCE

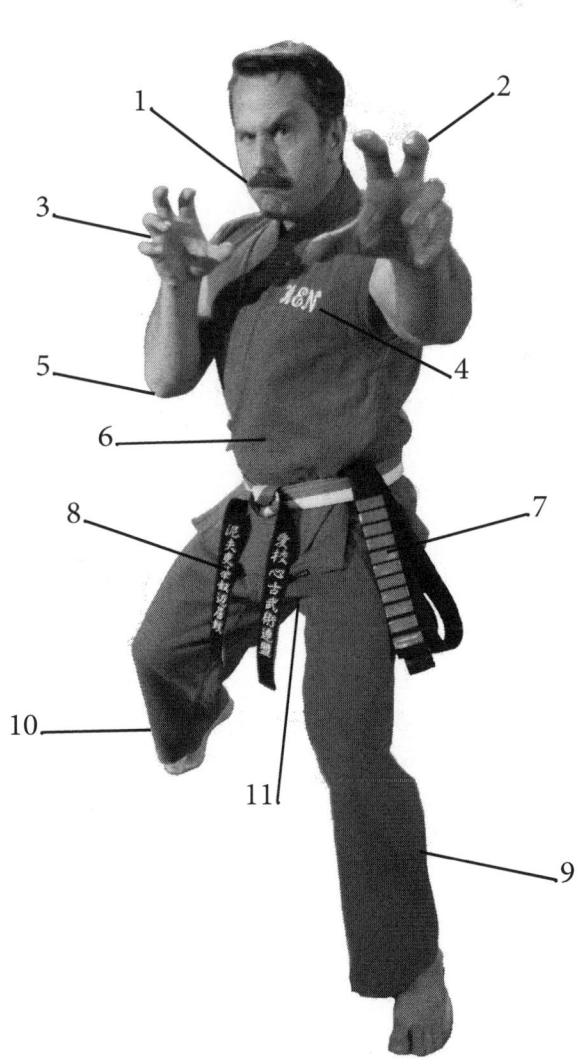

20

1. **Tactical Mustache:** soaks up blood while biting opponent.

2. **Front Tiger Claw:** for eye gouging.

3. **Rear Tiger Claw:** for catching punches.

4. **Name Embroidery:** so that survivors may tell the tale.

5. **Elbows:** for protecting ribs and leaning on dinner tables.

6. **Rock Hard Abs:** insulated with 22% body fat storage for fuel.

7. **11th Degree Black Belt:** to establish dominance by rank.

8. **Master's Belt:** to confuse opponent with mysterious language.

9. **Front Leg:** a coiled spring for stomping the groin.

10. **Rear Leg:** the fleshy sledgehammer for Restomping the Groin.

11. **Hips/Groin:** both vital components to the Thrust of Freedom.

KRAV MAGA IS BULLSHIT

REASON #1

It's "Non-Competitive".

Wikipedia describes Krav Maga as a "non-competitive" martial art which puts it in the same category as snowshoeing, choreographed swimming and hula hooping.

REASON #2

They Wear Shoes.

Krav Maga schools actually encourage their students to wear shoes while training. This negates the possibility of proper foot conditioning but it must be helpful when they are losing a fight and it's time to run away.

REASON #3

They Wear Patches.

Many Krav Maga schools still refuse to use the belt system and instead prefer issuing their students patches for each promotion. That means the only difference between Krav Maga students and Girl Scouts is that the Girl Scouts make better cookies.

REASON #4

The Name is Stupid.

In Hebrew the term "Krav Maga" literally translates to

"Contact Combat" which is redundant. That's like saying I'm going to foot-kick you in the ball-groin and then have some mouth-food before I take a sleep-nap.

REASON #5

It's Too Easy to Become an Instructor.

Recently I saw an advertisement that claimed anyone could become a certified Krav Maga instructor in just 10 days. Meanwhile it still takes 2 weeks of training to become a security guard at Wal-Mart.

REASON #6

It's Not a Battle Tested System.

Krav Maga is the official martial art of the Israeli military. I'll take fighting advice from the Israeli military as soon as they win a war. Like a World War. Not these little skirmishes. Saying Krav Maga prepares you for war is like saying food fights prepare you for culinary school.

REASON #7

It's Popular With Losers.

Many people drawn to Krav Maga have failed at learning other more challenging and complicated martial arts systems. But Krav Maga's limited curriculum makes it the G.E.D. of self defense training. G.E.D. is this case stands for Gave (up) Every (other) Discipline.

FINGER POINTING DEFENSE
a.k.a.
"BREAK THE FINGER"

There's nothing more American than the Preemptive Strike. In Ameri-Do-Te we don't wait for an attacker to put his fists in the air. If there is a threat we drop them like a bad habit. So, let's address a very common threatening motion that often precedes a violent physical altercation: The Finger Point.

Say some yahoo who thinks his name is Tommy Tough Guy walks up and jabs his finger in your chest.

Here's what you do...

Once the threat is clearly initiated (which is very important for legal reasons) you're going to secure the wrist. Then...

...BREAK THE FINGER.**

**The fewer fingers you grab the more control you will have. Think of it as a joystick for your attacker. Except it causes pain. So... it's more like a pain-stick. Know how to pop and pull that pain-stick.

Break the Wrist.

Break the Arm.

Smash the Groin.

Break the Nose.

Sweep the Leg.

Do NOT Break the Fall!

Knee-Drop the Pelvis.

Kick the Head.

STOMP THE HEAD**

**Walk on gravel whenever possible and stop washing your feet to make stomping more devastating.

Stomp the Throat.

Kick the Neck

Then... As always...

RESTOMP THE GROIN!

Then Exit Out.

AMERI-DO-TE WORD SEARCH

```
A N D H E U D M F I S H H O O K T M
T G S M C B A B W I N D K E B Q O R
U H R B C M M H P L T P R U U T S B
F K R H W B E A M D I I Q Y L E T E
M C N U D J R L O P H S C W L A T Q
A H K D S T I J T K S B A F S T Y W
S G E K F T D B S J L G O P H I U U
T S R Q C W O R E C A F L L I K J A
E D S L A L T F R L U U E R T C I G
R N E A L V E M F H B T Y H R T P R
K 8 Y S Y I U Q X R E X B T V U Y O
E R H C A M E D R A E W V B H Y Q I
N I K N U C G V P M O E D T C I U N
O T O D D W O O D L A N D B Q R H G
Y N Z M W M W E R O N J N O Z B T R
W E B T I H S L L U B W O V M N G A
M H E I Y G N U A M I O V H Q D N B
```

In Ameri-Do-Te it's important to condition your brain. Make yourself smarter by trying out this word search. You will recognize more techniques and people if you are familiar with my show "Enter The Dojo" on YouTube.

www.youtube.com/EnterTheDojoShow

31

NEVER PROMOTE A STUDENT IF THEY'RE NOT READY
a.k.a.
THE PURPLE BELT INCIDENT

I once had a teenage student who wanted to test for purple belt before he was ready. I had reservations about it but his mother was pressuring me and I'd already cashed the check for his testing fee. So, I let him test. He screwed up on a couple of things but I thought "That's okay. I'll just fix those problems down the road." But I never got the chance.

The next day the student was so proud of his new belt that he decided to wear it to school and show it off on the playground. Ended up showing it to a couple of meth heads over by the dumpster and those two junkies decided to throw him a beating. They hit him with a lead pipe. Stomped on him. Used their cigarettes to set his clothes on fire. Then urinated on him to put the fire out.

I get an angry call from his mother blaming me for what happened. She said I passed him too early and gave him a false sense of security. And I'll tell you… I did feel responsible. For two days I sat at the hospital waiting for him to wake up and when he finally did I was the first person he saw. I looked him right in the eye… <u>then I took his purple belt away.</u> Gave it to somebody who deserved it.

I said "You can't go around getting your ass kicked if you're representing my school. If you're gonna fight you have to win." Some folks may consider that harsh. But you want to know the moral of that story?

A year later (after the surgery and physical therapy and all that nonsense) the same student came back to my dojo and tested for Purple again.

Unfortunately he still failed. After the beating he took, his hands were all… you know…(see picture below)

He couldn't do the moves. That's not my fault.

33

BECOME LETHAL BY ASSOCIATION

If you're currently studying some bullshit martial art you most likely already belong to one of the hundreds of martial arts "associations" around the world. If you study Kenpo it's probably the A.K.K.S. If you study Taekwondo it's the W.T.F.** The problem is these organizations exist only to line the pockets of a select few who run the organization and they abuse the loyalty of students and school owners to do so.

I know that some of you who purchase this book already study my instructional videos at ameridote.com and while I appreciate your dedication… you're not doing it right. From what I've seen your Kill Faces aren't lethal enough, your Thrust of Freedom lacks penetration and when you do your Hurticanes you're only hurting yourselves.

That's why I believe there must be some sort of standard that we can all hold ourselves to.

So I've created the only martial arts organization you'll ever have to join. It's called:

Maintain **Y**our **A**meri-Do-Te **S**treet **S**kills… or for short:

M.Y.A.S.S.

**which is appropriate considering that's what I said when I saw Taekwondo for the first time: "WTF is this Bullshit?"

Let me tell you something. If you're serious about learning Ameri-Do-Te…

You NEED to be in M.Y.A.S.S.

While other martial arts organizations charge hefty ongoing registration fees year after year, M.Y.A.S.S. has a one-time entry fee of $10. Unlike those faceless organizations that are often cold and uncaring I think you'll find M.Y.A.S.S. to be a warm and welcoming environment.**

One of the main benefits of joining this organization is that once you're inside you won't be alone. I've got Karate people in M.Y.A.S.S. I've got Krav Maga people in M.Y.A.S.S. I've got Brazilian Jiu Jitsu people in M.Y.A.S.S. In fact, just last week I managed to fit 15 Filipino Stick Fighters in M.Y.A.S.S. (which wasn't easy, believe me.)

Join Today by sending $10 to: Master Ken P.O. BOX 67495 Albuquerque, NM 87913

**If you don't believe me just ask Todd. He was the first member to be in M.Y.A.S.S. and he speaks very highly of it.

HOW TO BEAT A BOXER

There's an old saying that goes: "Never box a Boxer." There's another old saying that goes: "Don't drink the water in Mexico." Ignoring either of these sayings will have you leaking out of every orifice.

But what if a boxer squares off with you <u>outside</u> of the ring? Luckily there's a sure fire way to defeat a trained striker by using strategy.

If confronted by a Boxer it is best to fall back into a boxing stance. This will lead him to believe that you too are a trained striker and it will cause a moment of hesitation that you can exploit for your benefit.

Next, offer your wrist as a gesture. He won't be able to resist this trap of apparent surrender...

If he considers himself a Master of the Boxing Arts he will undoubtedly take the bait (I call this: "master-baiting") and now it is your chance to think outside the box...

Immediately execute a left inward/downward palm heel block while chambering the freed right hand. Then deliver a right punch to the solar plexus, rotating your body for added torque, while chambering your left hand.

Notice how far outside of the box I'm thinking. I'm not even thinking outside the box. I'm thinking outside the box-es. Plural. That means I thought so far outside the first box that the other boxes became... thought... out of... as well.

It's this kind of revolutionary thinking that has made me world renowned for my unpredictable techniques. Not even the famous boxing champion Mickey Mantle could've outsmarted this mind-bending technique.

Finish your opponent with a left elbow strike to the jaw, rattling his brain inside of his skull and causing him to fall to the ground for the obligatory groin-stomp and restomp.**

**Any questions?
If so, feel free to ask.
Just remember...**

You're talking to a book.

**Every Ameri-Do-Te technique ends with a groin being stomped and restomped. If it is not pictured, it's implied. This goes for my videos too. So stop sending me angry letters. I didn't even know people still wrote letters unless they were John Deere letters.

AIKIDO IS BULLSHIT

REASON #1

They Never Spar.

The entire philosophy of Aikido is based on harmony whether it be with nature or with the "energy" of your attacker, who could be a drug-crazed, bodybuilding, hatchet-wielding maniac for all we know. This philosophy does not prepare someone for real life combat. However, I will say that Ameri-Do-Te does have a technique in which we try to understand what is in our opponent's heart. We do this by ripping the heart out through their rib cage and looking at it.

REASON #2

They Dress Funny.

Once students reach black belt level they are required to wear a black skirt known as a "hakama". It is also rumored that the traditional way of wearing these is to go without undergarments of any kind. That way, when they fall down on the mat and their hakama flies up, the Sho-dan can Sho-U-His-Dong.

REASON #3

It's Designed to Fight People Wearing Armor.

The techniques that define Aikido were developed at a time when one's opponent was likely a samurai warrior dressed in armor up to their wrists. This is probably why most Aikido practitioners are experts in small joint manipulation. Small. Joint. Manip. Ulation.**

**Text here is extra small to match the size of your joint.

REASON #4

They Practice Falling Down. A Lot.

The success of their techniques requires one's training partner to have excellent "ukemi" which literally translates to "receiving self". It is the attacker's ukemi, not the defender's technique, that results in the dramatic break falling that most spectators find impressive.

Without good ukemi the art of Aikido would be lost. So they spend years training the best ways to help their attackers fall gracefully to the mat without physical harm. This makes the fight last far too long.

In Ameri-Do-Te we don't want our attackers to fall gracefully onto anything. That's why I don't train my students to throw people on to things. I train them to throw people off of things. Balconies. Escalators. Cruise Ships.

The Trampoline Store. Mainly because of the irony.

Because if you were to throw someone inside the trampoline store they would just bounce to safety. But if you go outside and throw them off the roof and they're looking in as they fall they'll think: Gosh... I wish I was falling in there.

Then *Splat*!

REASON #5

The Attacks are Unrealistic.

The scenarios against which Aikido students are taught to defend do not involve traditional kicks or punches but rather movements meant to mimic that of a sword attack… minus the sword. I hear that once the students reach black belt level they learn to defend themselves against the dreaded "finger pistol".

REASON #6

Steven Seagal.

EVERYTHING YOU'LL EVER NEED TO KNOW ABOUT WRIST GRAB DEFENSES

One of the most common moves taught in dojos is the two-hand wrist grab defense. That's because there are so many options for defending this attack. You can counter grab the wrist (above) into an inverted gooseneck lock... or you can attack pressure points** in the forearm.

**Targeting what Latin warriors refer to as: *Pressure Pointess Maximinus*

You can straighten your fingers, which expands the circumference of your wrist, weakening the attacker's grip, then reach down and pull your own hand out like a "hand-le".

Some of this instruction is so obvious, yet it enlightens the dark corners of your mind like a "cand-le".

A more complicated defense using "Tuite"** involves handing your wrist to yourself, then folding your fingers into your opponent, stretching the tendons in his wrist to their breaking point and causing intense pain.

**"Tuite" translates to "joint manipulation" which is a term often used in Japanese dojos and massage parlors.

You can counter grab the outside of your opponent's wrist and apply pressure to the elbow joint... blah blah blah. As you see there's a million fancy, complicated ways to escape the two-handed wrist grab.

But if you're in a hurry when someone grabs your wrist...

...and you don't have time for all that...

Just punch him in the face.

THE THRUST OF FREEDOM

What are the most common parts of your body that you use in a fight? Your hands? Your feet? Sure. But what if you break your hand or your foot and you still have to fight? Luckily there's a part of your body that involves over 17 different muscle groups that you can use to defend yourself:

YOUR HIPS.**

**The hips pictured are my hips. Not your hips.

There are four major directions in the Thrust of Freedom:

You can thrust left.

You can thrust right.

You can thrust back.

You can thrust front.

51

The Front Thrust will be the most commonly used version of the Thrust of Freedom in most self defense situations.

Practice this motion as often as you can. The more you practice, the more powerful the thrust...

This move is most effective if executed at a slightly upward angle like so:

45 Degrees (as the crow flies.)

1. Say some ruffian rolls up on you and applies a front bear hug without consent.

2. Place your hands on his hips and "cock" your thrust.

3. Apply a Front Thrust to his groin area. If you've been conditioning this part of your body by thrusting small trees or piles of sand this should cause him more pain than it causes you.

4. When he drops to a knee from intense pain make sure to align his head with your hips for a *second* Front Thrust...

5. Deliver a Front Thrust to the face.
This move will be the finishing blow!

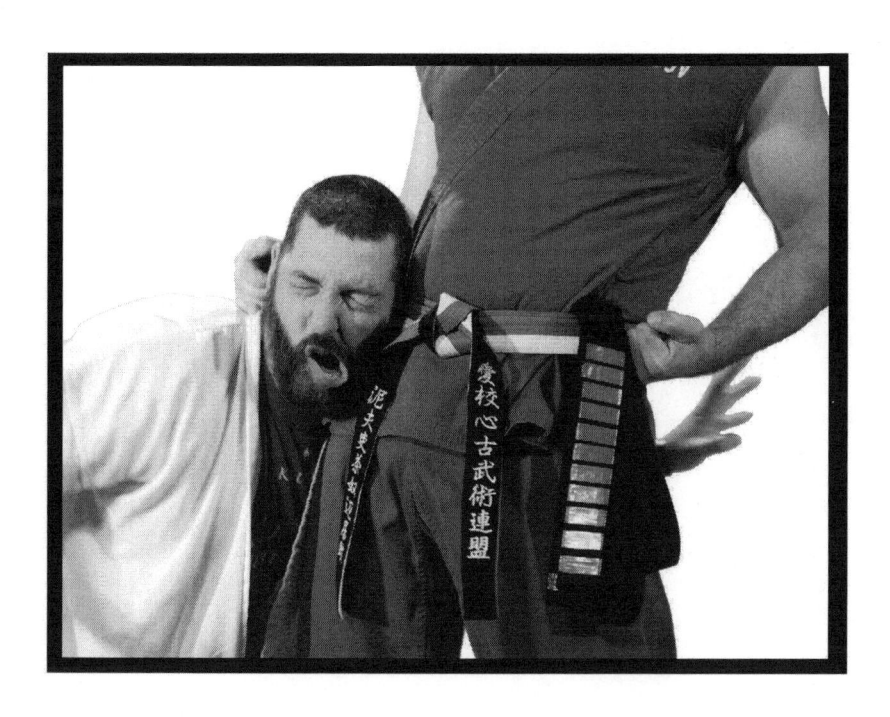

55

Whenever I teach the standing application of the T.O.F. people say "Master Ken! That's a perfect technique in a stand up fight... but what if I'm fighting on the ground?

Here's your answer:

Let's say you find yourself on top of your opponent in what those BJJ Bullshit practitioners call "Side Control".

With proper placement of your hands and a quick shift of the hips you can quickly move into a devastating position.

Trust me. He'll *never* see this coming!

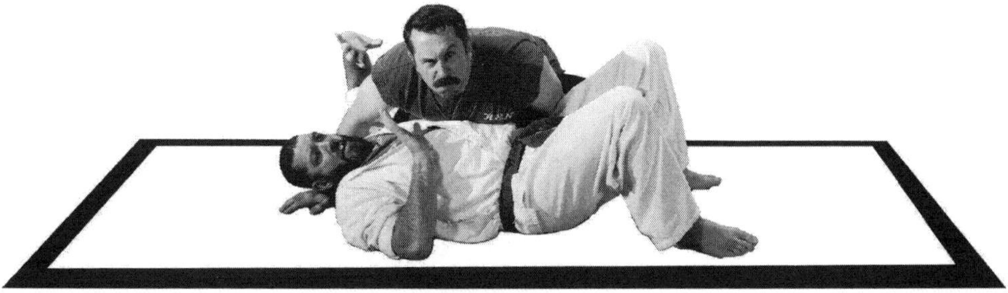
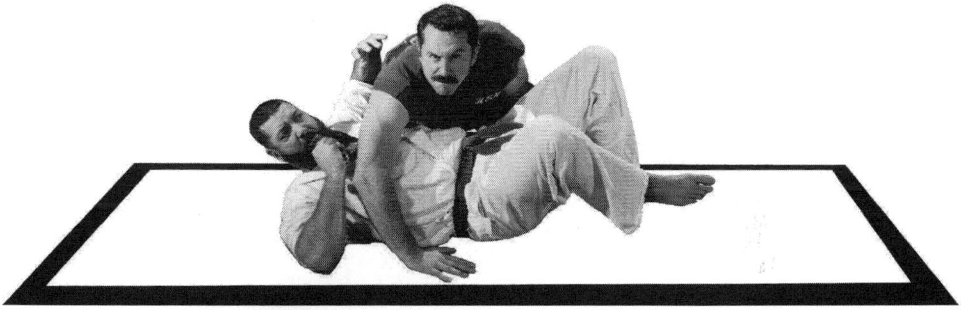
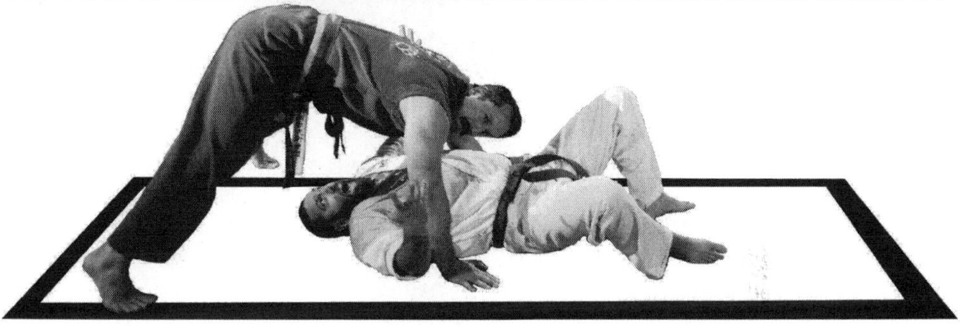
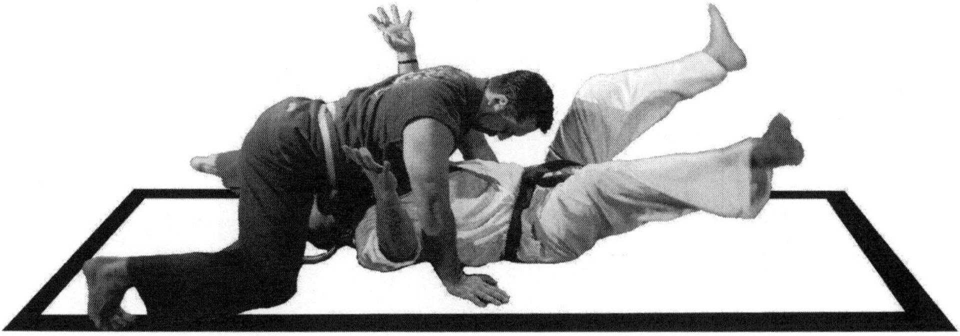

Add a headbutt to the groin...

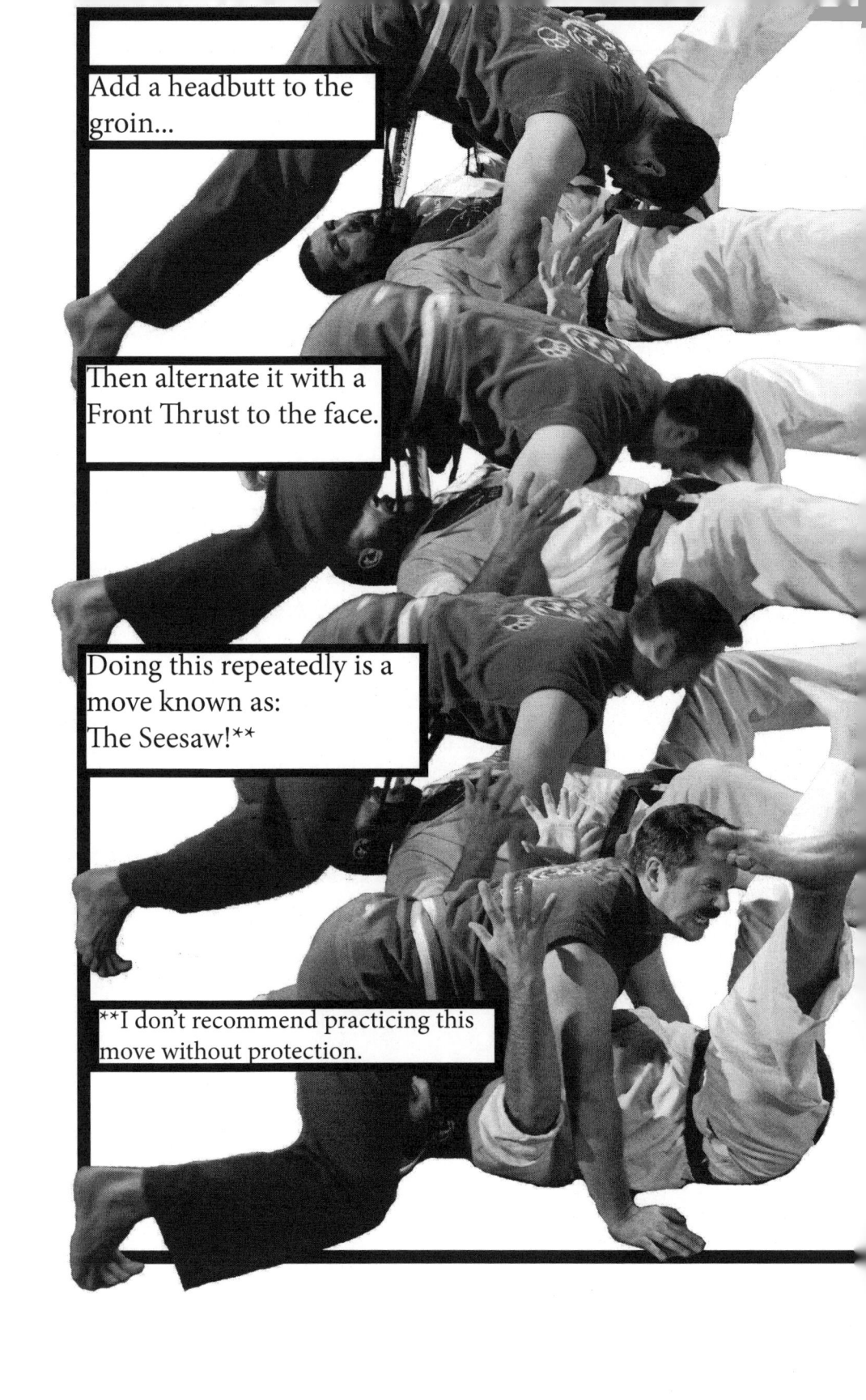

Then alternate it with a Front Thrust to the face.

Doing this repeatedly is a move known as: The Seesaw!**

**I don't recommend practicing this move without protection.

ANTI-GRAPPLING TECHNIQUES

*"I do not fear the shark
because I fight on land."*

- Master Ken

If there's one thing that chafes my hide it's the popularity of ground fighting. Back in my day we knew enough to stay off of the ground. And if we ended up there we didn't stay down for long. These days you have fighters who watch a couple hours of UFC and next thing you know they're jumping guard faster than a kangaroo on a trampoline.

That's why I've created a series of "anti-grappling" techniques to counteract the most common and most dangerous BJJ positions and submissions.

Because if you're one of these guys who's going to intentionally pull someone onto the ground out in the parking lot and get your head stomped into the asphalt... that's your own dumbass fault.

THE DOUBLE TAP

Brazilian Jiu Jitsu. Judo. Sambo. Greco Roman Wrestling. They all have submissions that once you find yourself in them are nearly impossible to get out of... unless you do one of two things:

1) Spend years learning a bunch of bullshit grappling techniques.

2) Learn the Ameri-Do-Te solution.

This move will unlock *any* submission! I call it the "skeleton key" of anti-grappling moves.

Let's say that you find yourself in the dreaded Triangle Choke** which cuts off both oxygen and blood circulation to the brain.

This choke was made famous by Royce Gracie in the original UFC. Little known fact: There is no "R" in the Brazilian alphabet. That's why Royce is pronounced "Hoyce". Rixon is pronounced "Hixon". And their word for sparring, which is called <u>rolling</u>, is pronounced "holing".

**The Triangle Choke actually got it's name due to the fact that it forces the opponent's nose far too close to the smelliest parts of any human body: the groin, the anus and the feet.

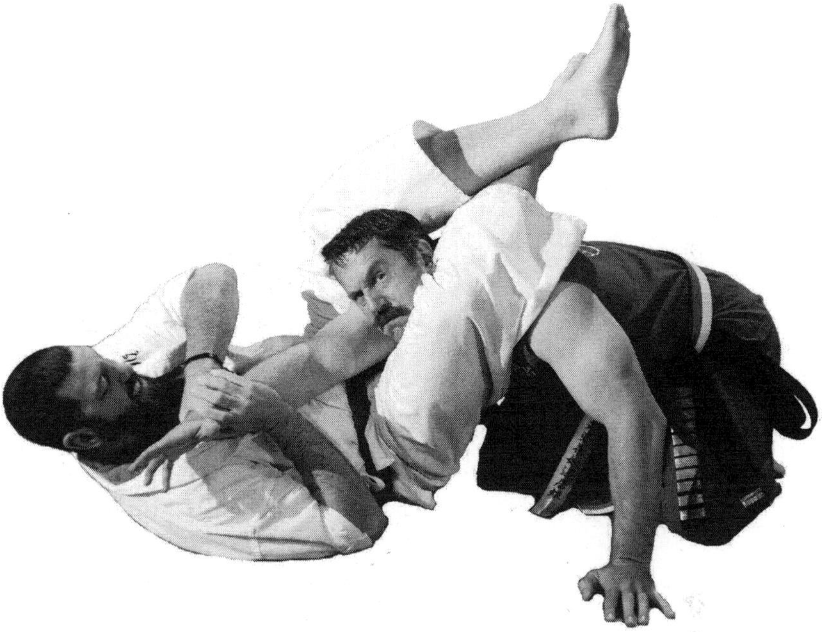

Quickly deliver two firm "taps" to the opponent's body to signal your implied surrender.

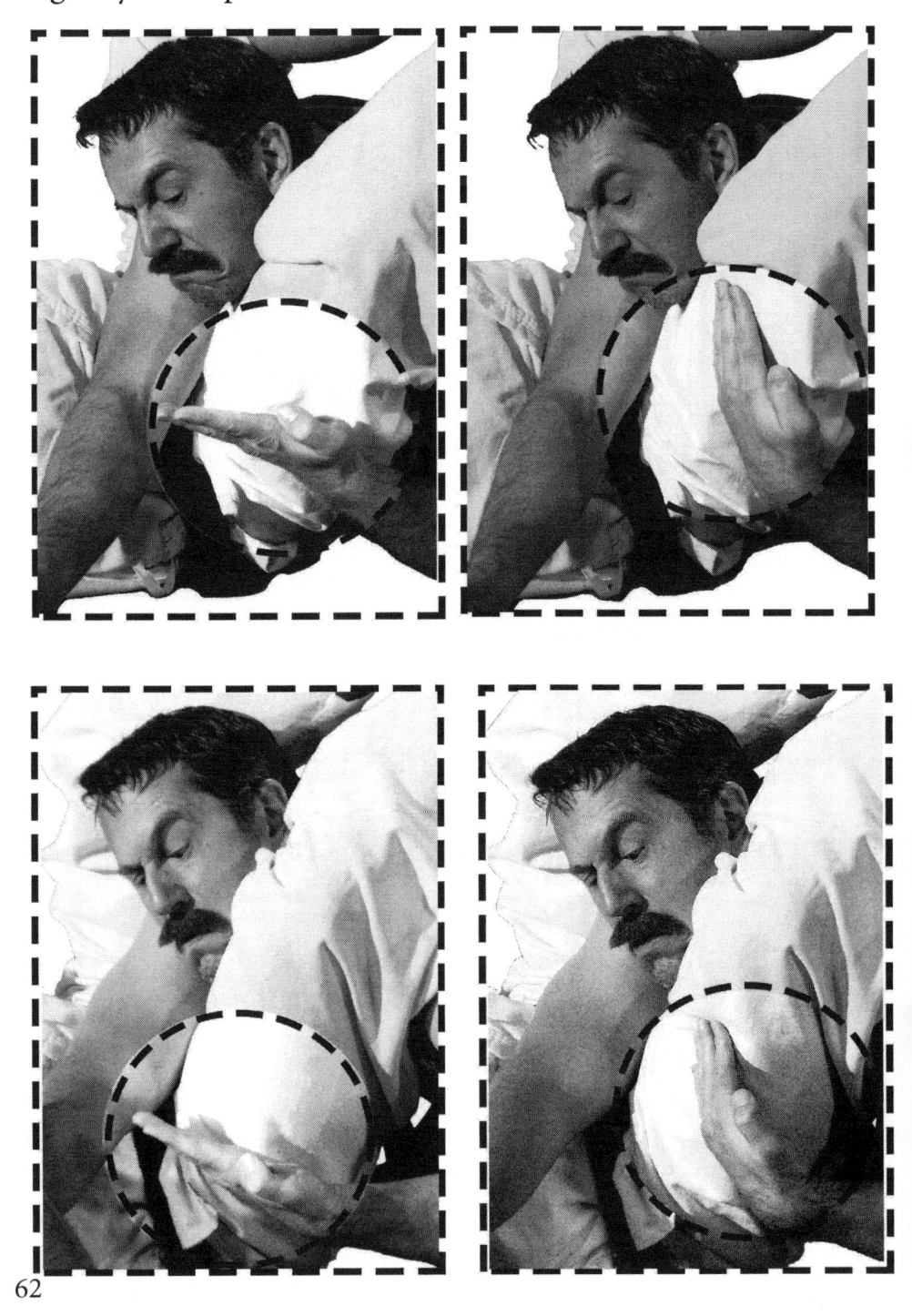

The moment he releases, it's time to finish him off. Deliver a headbutt to the face, then stand and pivot to Restomp the Groin and victory** is yours!

**This may get you disqualified in BJJ competition.

THE GAS CHAMBER

The most feared tactic in any combat situation is the use of chemical warfare. But that's because it's so effective. That's why I've added this technique** to Ameri-Do-Te.

**This is a modification on Javier Vazquez' technique called the Vazque-Fix. Just like sawing the barrel off of a shotgun makes it more deadly and illegal, I've sawed off the end of this technique to make it "Street Lethal".

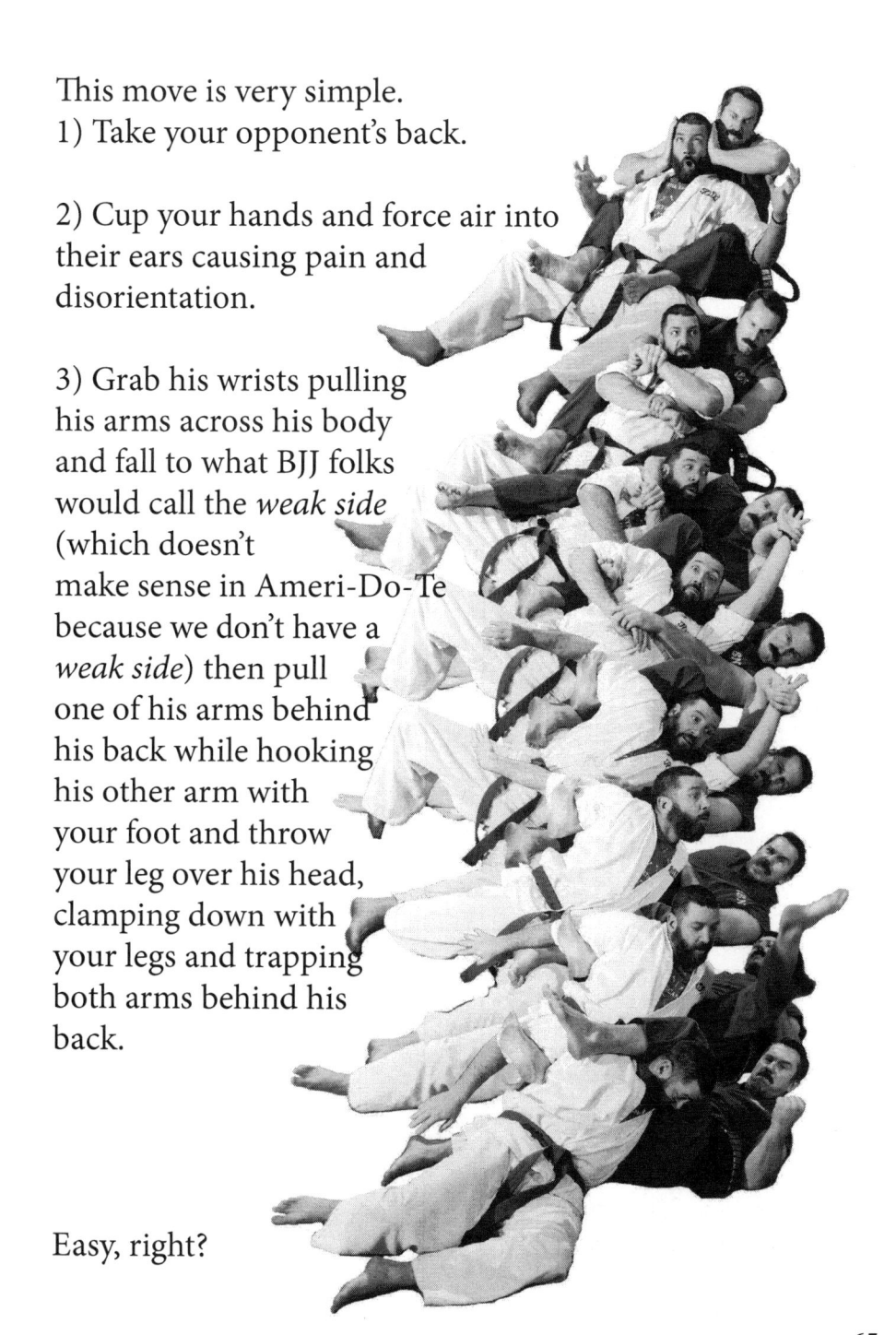

This move is very simple.
1) Take your opponent's back.

2) Cup your hands and force air into their ears causing pain and disorientation.

3) Grab his wrists pulling his arms across his body and fall to what BJJ folks would call the *weak side* (which doesn't make sense in Ameri-Do-Te because we don't have a *weak side*) then pull one of his arms behind his back while hooking his other arm with your foot and throw your leg over his head, clamping down with your legs and trapping both arms behind his back.

Easy, right?

At this point it's time to release your natural gas reserves which will suffocate your opponent.

I forgot to mention one very important step: preparation.

This move is only effective if your system is fully loaded with as much methane gas as possible. This can be accomplished by eating baked beans, Chinese egg rolls, raisins, cabbage, garlic... preferably all in the same meal. In a matter of hours your gastrointestinal system should be sufficiently toxic.

It may also be helpful to wear a gas mask to protect yourself from your own attack as a quick shift in wind direction could leave you subject to your own weapon.

This is age old advice from the famous philosopher Flachu Lance who once said:

> *"He who smelt it, dealt it."*

THE HEART ATTACK

My biggest complaint about techniques from the guard is that they tend to be competition-based instead of street-based, focusing on moves that score points in competition. As everyone knows, there are no "points" in the street.

This guard technique ignores the normal rules of engagement and goes right to the "heart" of the matter. Let's say your opponent is attempting to punch you in the head or body.

Catch your opponent's punch.

Open your guard and <u>Sit Up...</u>

Break the neck!

This will cause temporary or permanent paralysis making your opponent's body easier to manipulate.

Reach down their throat and grab your opponent's heart.

Pull the heart out of his body.

Put the heart someplace where you won't forget it.

Flip your opponent onto his back being careful not to squish his recently extracted organ.

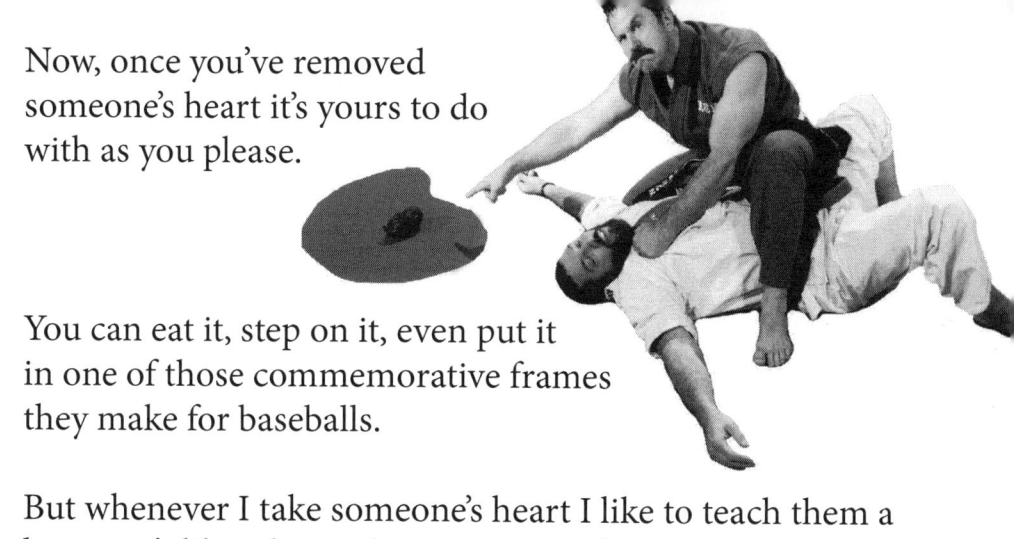

Now, once you've removed someone's heart it's yours to do with as you please.

You can eat it, step on it, even put it in one of those commemorative frames they make for baseballs.

But whenever I take someone's heart I like to teach them a lesson. It's like when a dog messes on the carpet. If you don't show it to him he's never going to learn.

So whenever I remove someone's heart I look him right in the eye and yell:

NO! NO!

KENPO IS BULLSHIT

REASON #1

Too Much Choreography.

Self Defense scenarios in Kenpo are known for being so intricate that your attacker must also know Kenpo in order for you to finish the technique. Which means Kenpo is basically a dance class but with fewer moves to memorize. While this may not be helpful in a street fight it does prepare students to be contestants on Dancing With The Stars.

REASON #2

The Techniques Have Stupid Names.

It's already difficult enough to remember the Japanese terminology for roundhouse kick is "Mawashi Geri" or that an outside block is "Soto Uke". How are students supposed to remember the difference between techniques called "Unfurling Crane" or "Sword of Destruction". If you're going that far with names then I'm going to start calling Kenpo "The Art of Too Many Moves With Stupid Names That Don't Work in The Street Anyway So Why Bother."

REASON #3

They Slap Themselves.

Supposedly many moves in Kenpo can't make contact with the training partner because they're too dangerous, so those strikes become slaps, many of which the Kenpo stylist hits him or herself with. For every time a Kenpo stylist hits their opponent, they hit themselves three times. Which is great because if you fight a Kenpo black belt long enough he'll kick his own ass.

REASON #4

It Uses Phony Science.

Kenpo claims to take a "scientific" approach to street fighting. But to my knowledge none of the techniques have ever been subject to the scientific method of making an observation, formulating a hypothesis and conducting an experiment.

For Example:

Observation: This gang member is wielding a switchblade and threatening to "cut" me.

Hypothesis: If he attacks he will end up being in extreme pain.

Conduct Experiment: Divert the stabbing attack, disarm him and take the knife, inserting the blade into his anus.

Result: Judging from the screaming, bleeding and pleading my hypothesis was correct.

REASON #5

They're Overweight.

For some reason the more stripes there are on a Kenpo black belt the bigger the belly is on the so-called "Master". Every degree of black belt must have double the calories or something because there seems to be a required weight gain. I was going to include a picture of the top ten Kenpo black belts in the world but the photograph alone weighs over 1500 lbs.

(Photo too heavy to include here.)

REASON #6

There Are Too Many Masters.

Kenpo has more 10th Degree Black Belts than any style in the world. It's too easy to get certified with stories of some people paying large sums of money to acquire rank at early ages. I don't have any respect for it but hey, if you want to shell out a few hundred bucks I'll sell you a 5th degree Kenpo Black Belt right now. Mail your check or money order to:

Enter The Dojo Show/Riffraff New Media
P.O. Box 67495 Albuquerque, NM 87193

ILLEGAL TECHNIQUES

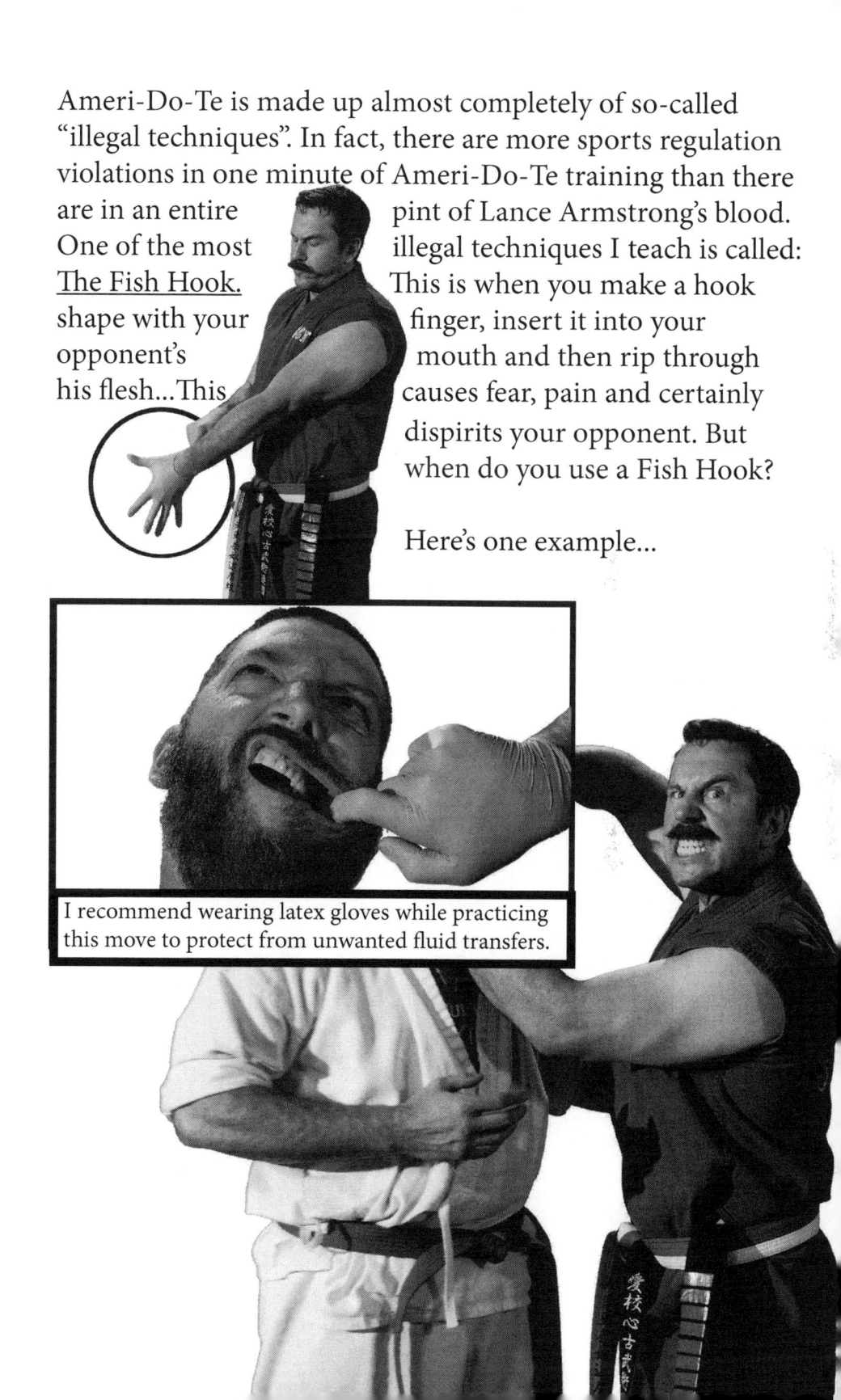

Ameri-Do-Te is made up almost completely of so-called "illegal techniques". In fact, there are more sports regulation violations in one minute of Ameri-Do-Te training than there are in an entire pint of Lance Armstrong's blood. One of the most illegal techniques I teach is called: The Fish Hook. This is when you make a hook shape with your finger, insert it into your opponent's mouth and then rip through his flesh...This causes fear, pain and certainly dispirits your opponent. But when do you use a Fish Hook?

Here's one example...

I recommend wearing latex gloves while practicing this move to protect from unwanted fluid transfers.

Let's say that Todd here is a pickpocket and he decides to steal my wallet. The moment I feel his hand on my glutes I'm going to pin it to my body to keep him from getting away!

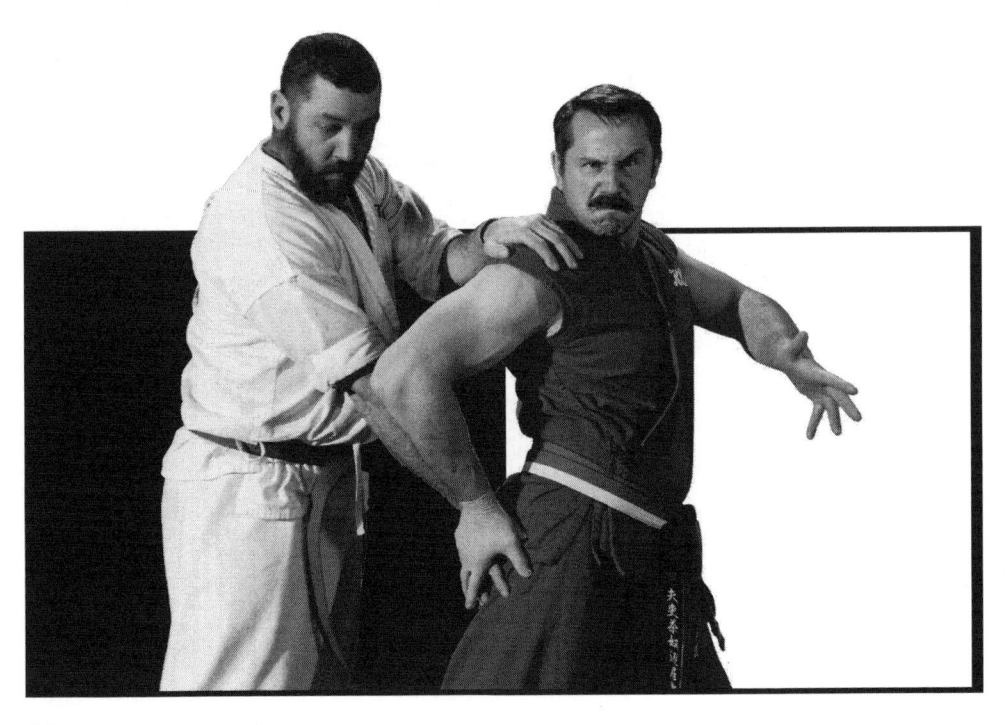

Now as you can see if I turn into him I have to invert my Fish Hook which isn't as efficient.

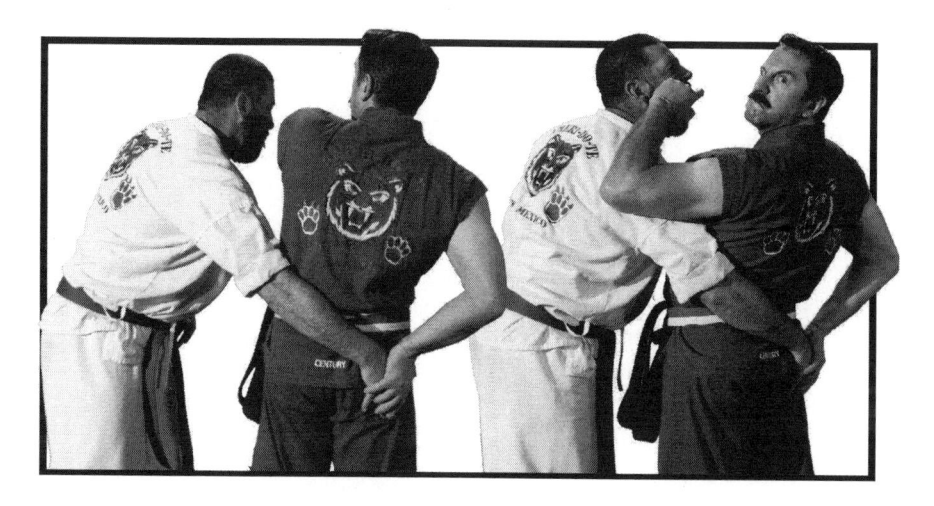

That's why I would do what's called a "Reach Around". I'm going to reach around the opponent and insert my Fish Hook into his mouth.

Now, while one Fish Hook may be sufficient why not use <u>two</u> Fish Hooks to ensure that this never happens again?

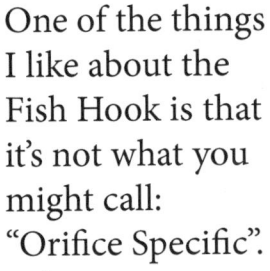

One of the things I like about the Fish Hook is that it's not what you might call: "Orifice Specific". Wherever you can fit it... it will work. That's why I'd put the second Fish Hook in the anus.

Just know that I can tear him in half from this position.

Once you insert the second Fish Hook they tend to cry, apologize and even give you your wallet back.

In the event of a total surrender...

...take the second Fish Hook out of the anus...

...and just go for the mouth.

THE HURTICANE

One thing that most martial arts don't address properly is the issue of multiple attackers. Sooner or later it's something you're going to have to deal with. It's a statistical reality that 1 in 5 people will be attacked by 5 or more people.

That's why I've developed a technique that if executed properly can make you equal to up to 10 men... or 14 dwarves.

I call it: The Hurticane.

Basically you need to throw every technique you've ever learned in every direction as fast and hard as you can at the same time.

Punching, kicking, pinching, clawing...and biting. Don't forget to bite.

I've included a visual representation of the Hurticane on the next page.

It's tough stuff so if this is your first time seeing it...

...you might want to hang on to something.

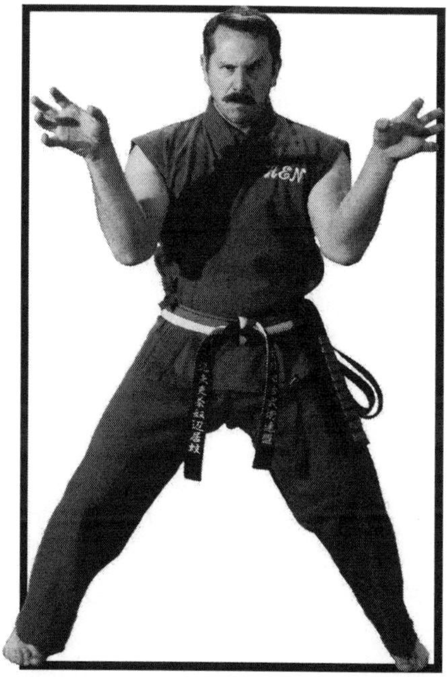

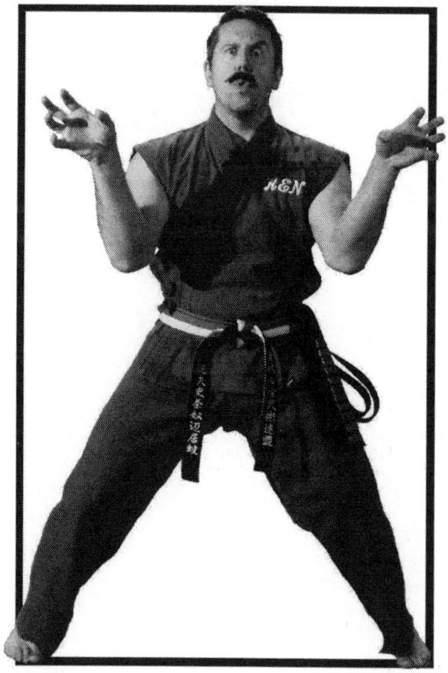

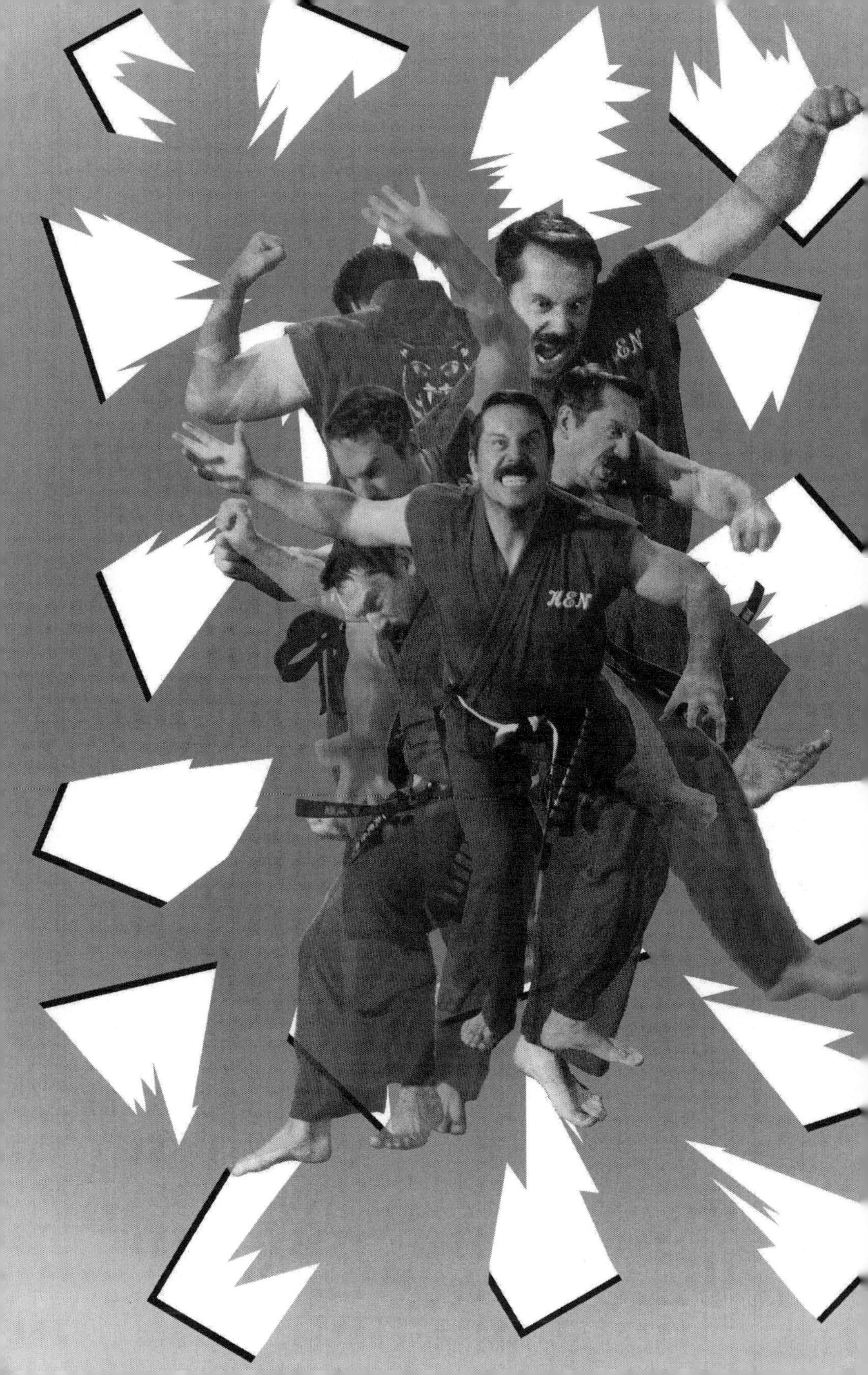

WEAPONS DEFENSES

*"I do not fear the weapon. For I am the weapon.
If you attack me with a weapon and I take your weapon
then I am a weapon holding a weapon. So I become
a weapon-weapon. Ever notice that if you say a word like
'weapon' enough times it stops sounding like a word?
Weaponweaponweaponweapon. See what I mean?"*

- Master Ken

Most knife defenses are "blade afraid": afraid of the blade. But in Ameri-Do-Te we teach you to embrace the blade. Literally.

That's why I've created a defensive technique that I call:

CREASE CONTROL

Bait your attacker by exposing a major artery. If he is a master of knife fighting this would be called "Master-Baiting".** When involved in life or death combat your skin begins to sweat. Once a cold blade makes contact with hot sweat you have a split second to create an airtight seal with the crease of your

By clamping down on the blade you neutralize the threat and your attacker can't get his weapon back!

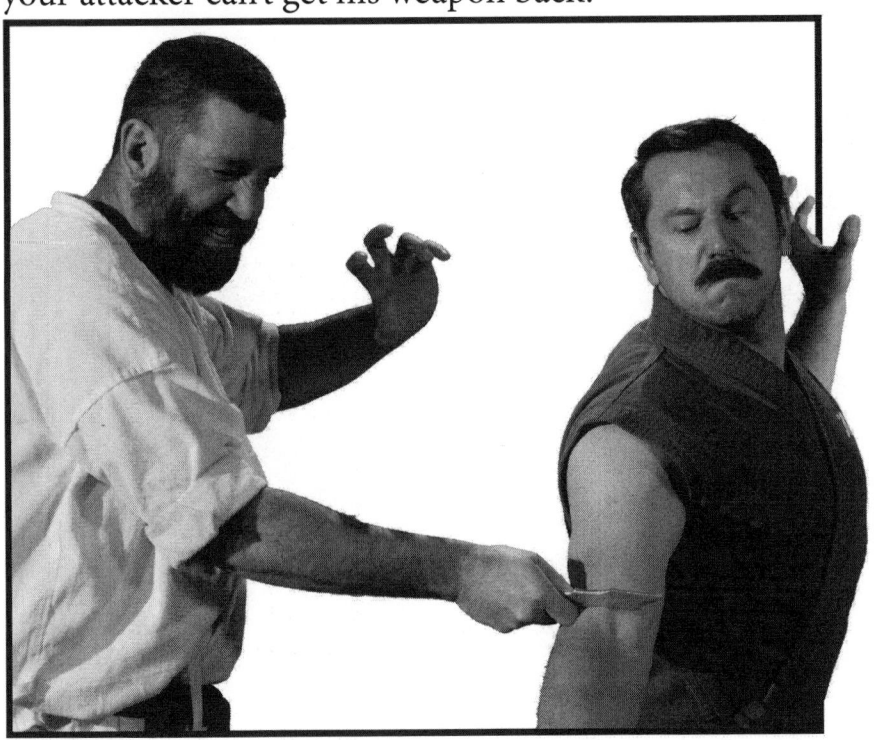

**mic check...in case you missed it the first time.

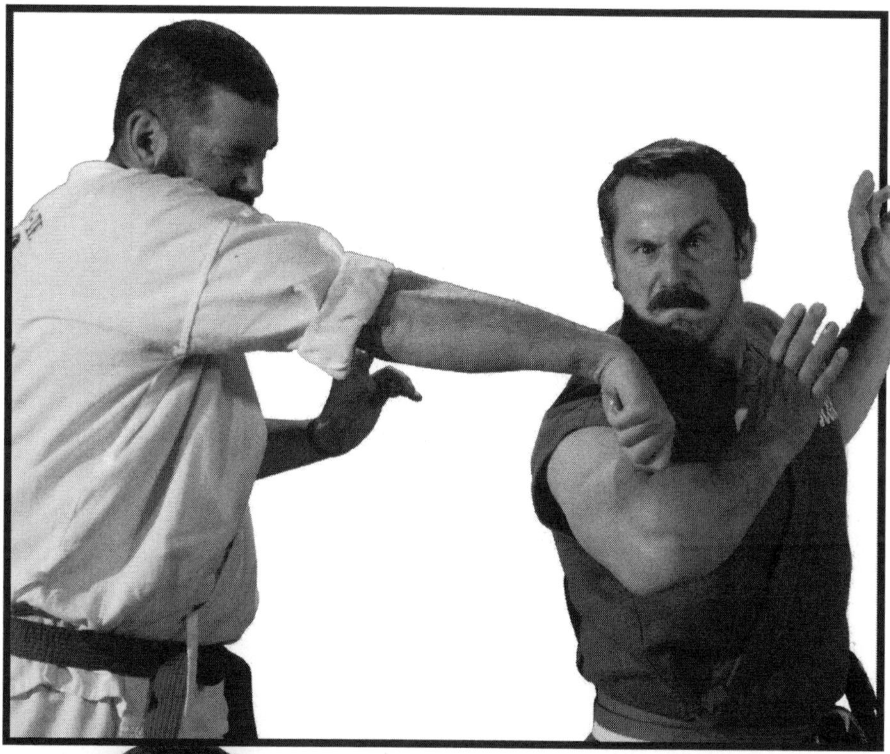

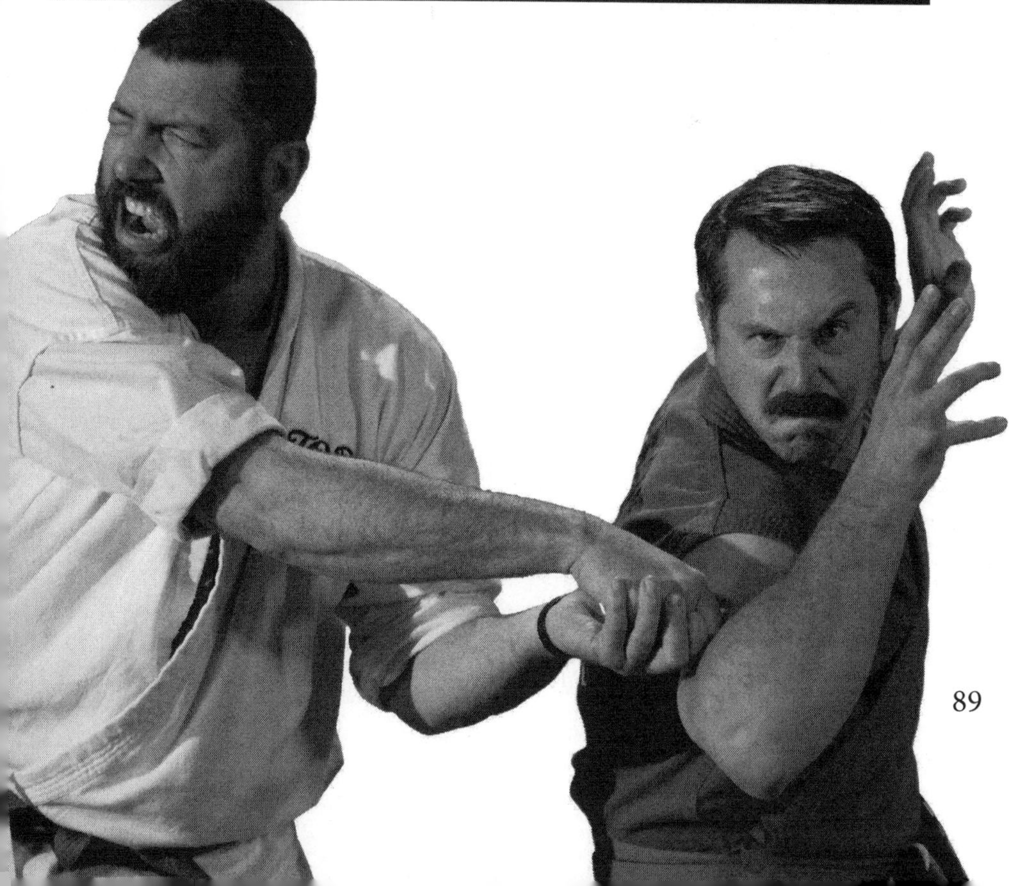

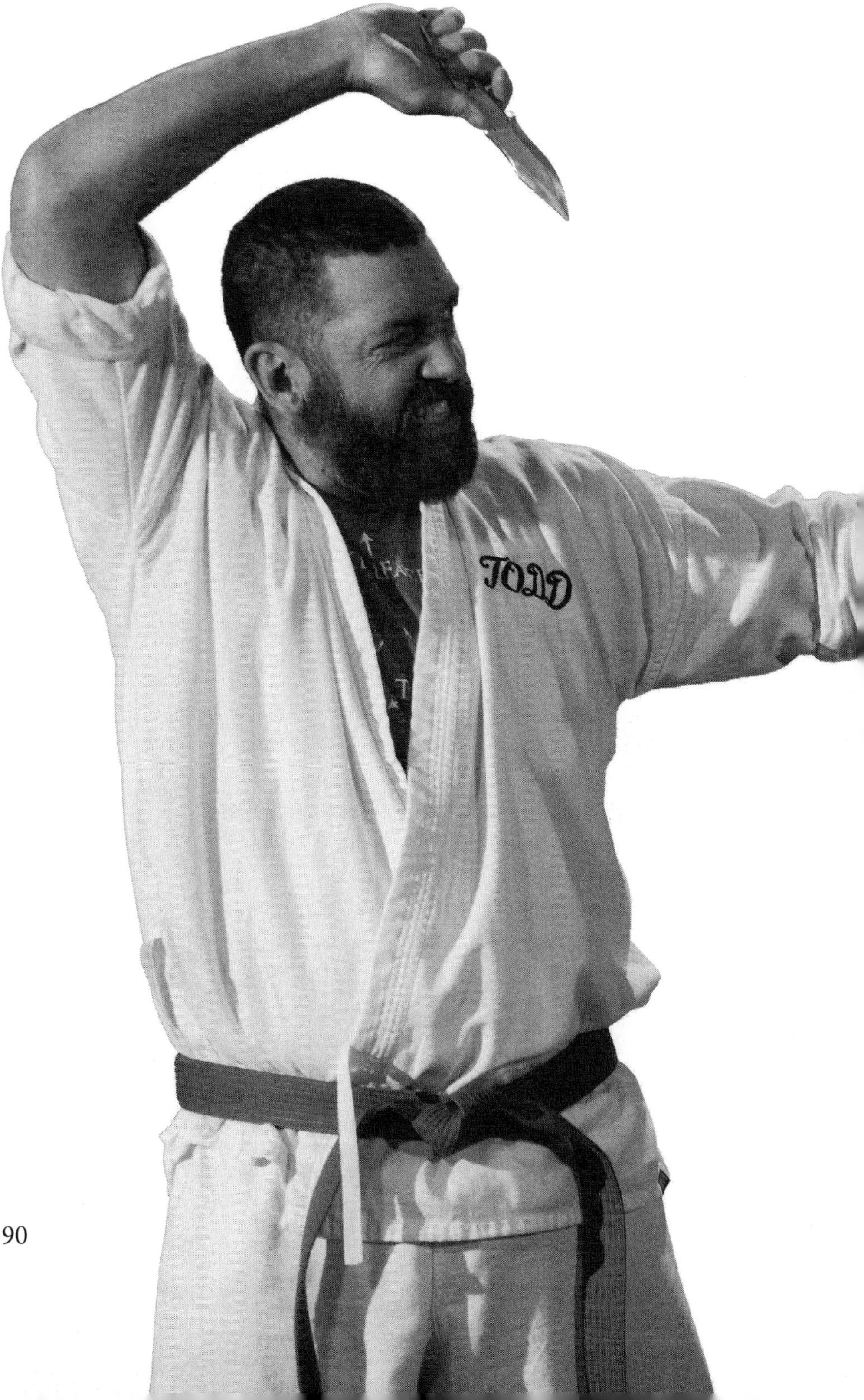
TODD

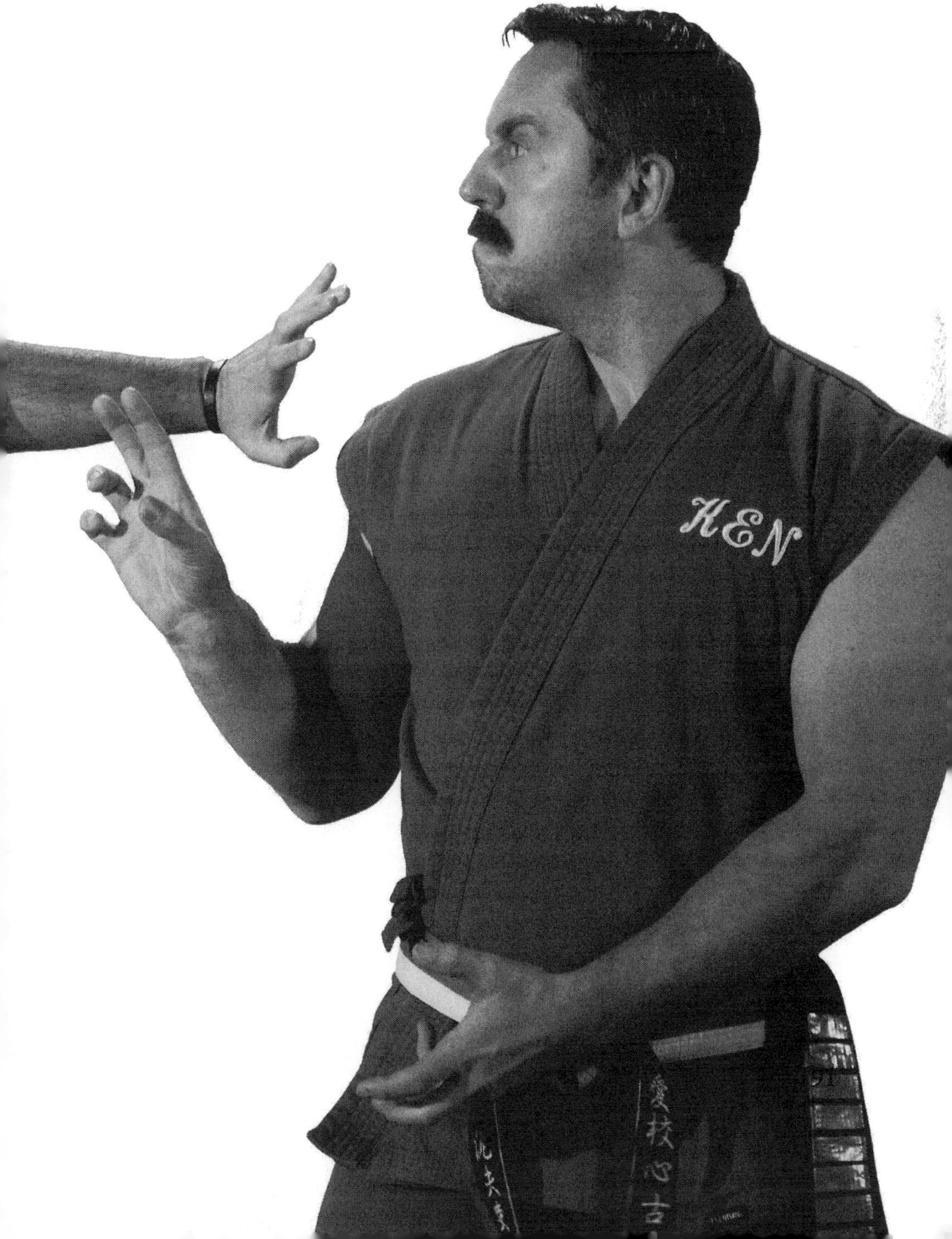
KEN

92

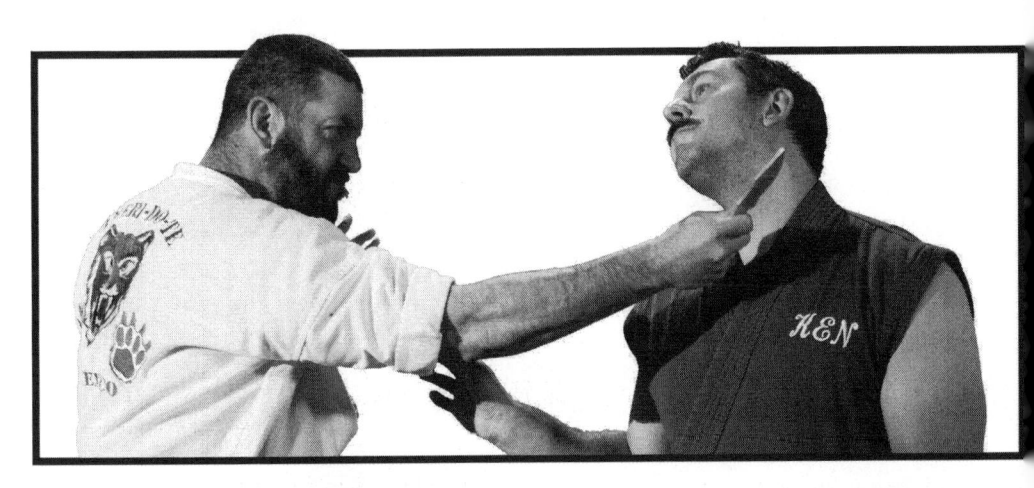

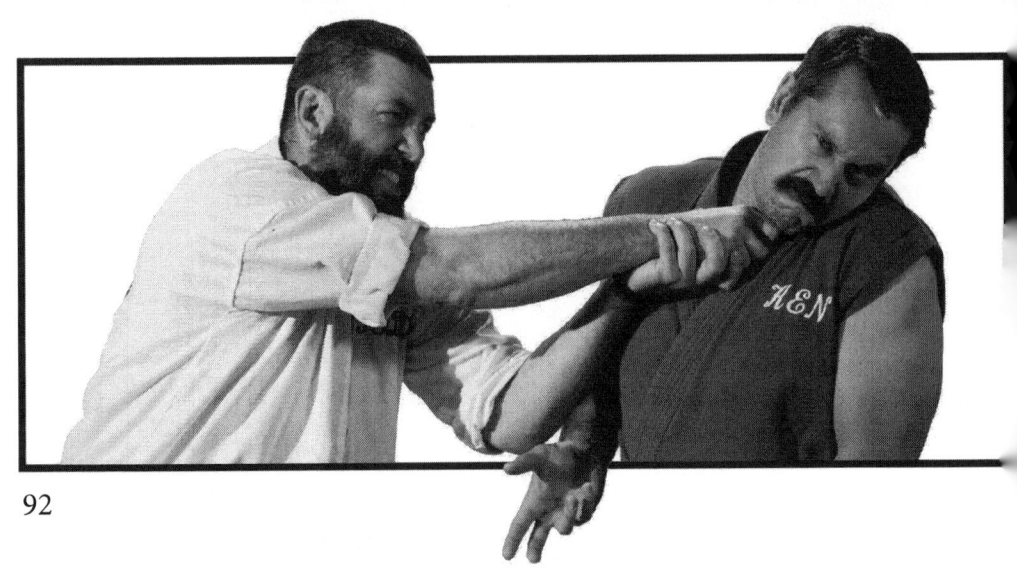

You can even use Crease Control to defend an attack from the rear!

93

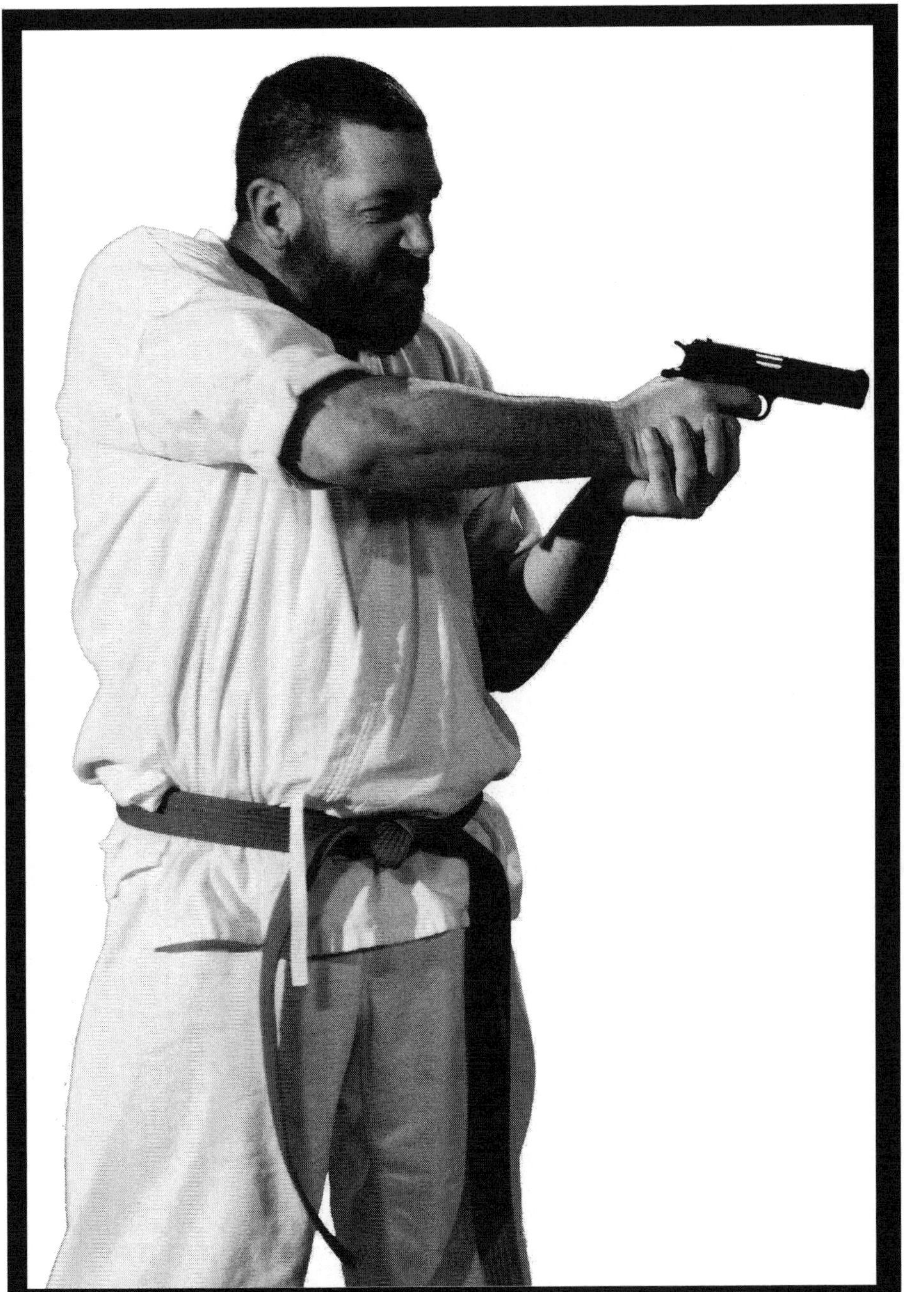

GUN DEFENSE

Most people don't realize that guns, just like people, function on oxygen.

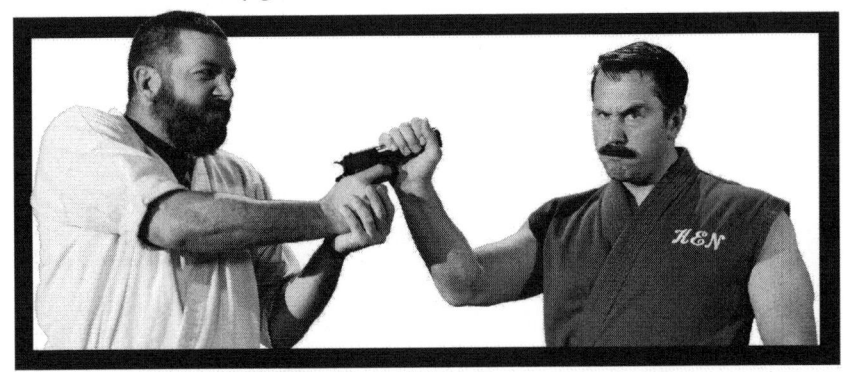

After grabbing the gun barrel to move it offline, take the tip of your finger...

...and plug the barrel with it. This will prevent the gun from firing.

You can also grab the gun with both hands to control it.

But don't extend your arms and move the weapon away from your body.

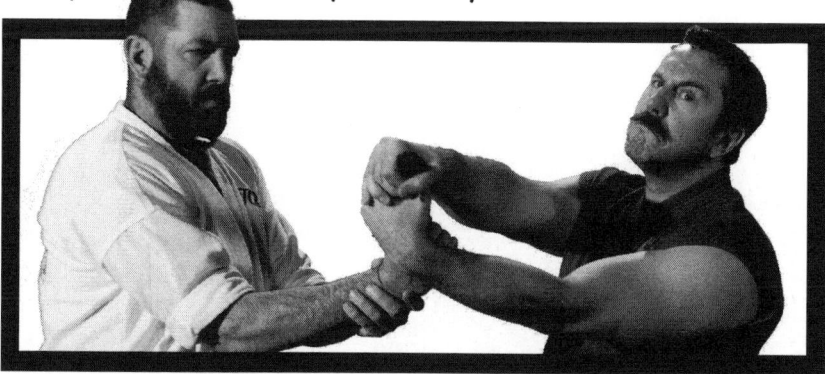

You'll have more control if you keep the gun *dead center*.

But how can you free up your hands to do some damage while maintaining control over the weapon? Here's your answer: Stuff the gun *between your thighs*. They are much stronger than your arms anyway.

This will leave your tiger claws free to remove the eyes while simultaneously breaking the neck.

99

Once you've removed his eyes and broken his neck, the corpse will fall and his grip will weaken, leaving the gun tucked safely below your genitals.

WHEN TO BRING A KNIFE TO A GUN FIGHT

There's an old saying that goes: "Never bring a knife to a gun fight." In some cases... I disagree.

It is good to bring one or more knives to fight an attacker with a firearm. So, I'm going to have Todd point the gun at me and tell him to fire...

BANG!

Not yet.

You'll see if I execute this technique quickly and effectively that *when* he fires...

BANG!

Not. Yet.

You'll soon see how effective a knife vs. gun scenario can be.

103

So, let's say Todd here points a firearm in my general direction. I happen to have TWO KNIVES in my possession at that exact moment.

Maybe he's attacking me in my kitchen.

Maybe I'm a sushi chef at a restaurant that's being robbed.

Maybe I own a knife store.

I could also be a blacksmith... that just made these two knives...

...anyway try not to overthink this part.

In one smooth motion I divert the gun away from my vital organs while severing the radial artery and punching him in the solar plexus with the butt end of the other knife like so...

I then cut up the sternum with one knife while checking the wrist of the gun hand with the other.

I may also choose to remove the section of his neck just below the windpipe. This is known as the "mastoid process".**

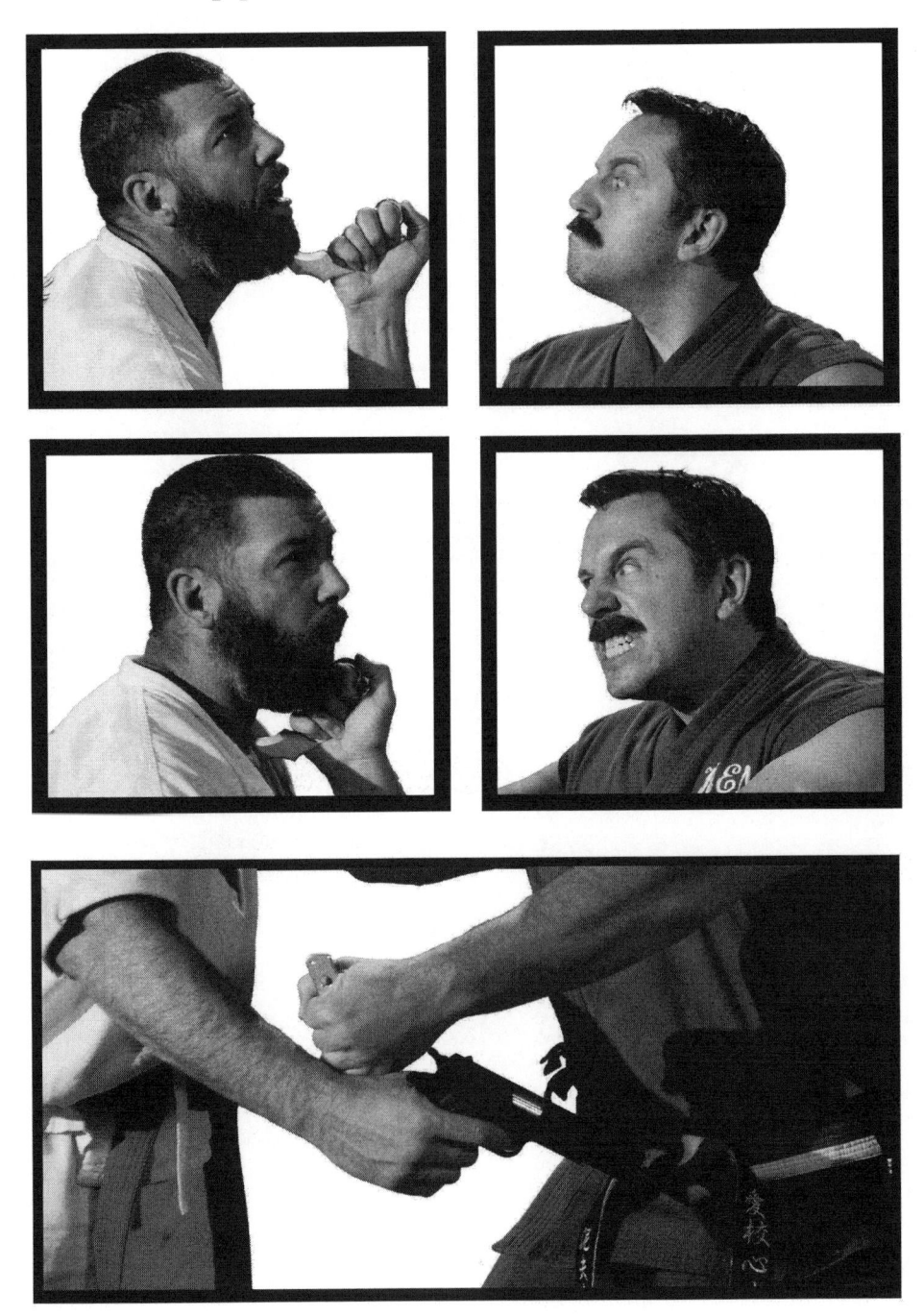

**May not be medically accurate.

In one motion, cut the carotid artery with one knife while cutting the gun out of the gun hand with the second knife.

Spin your opponent into what is known as a "Bladed Headlock".

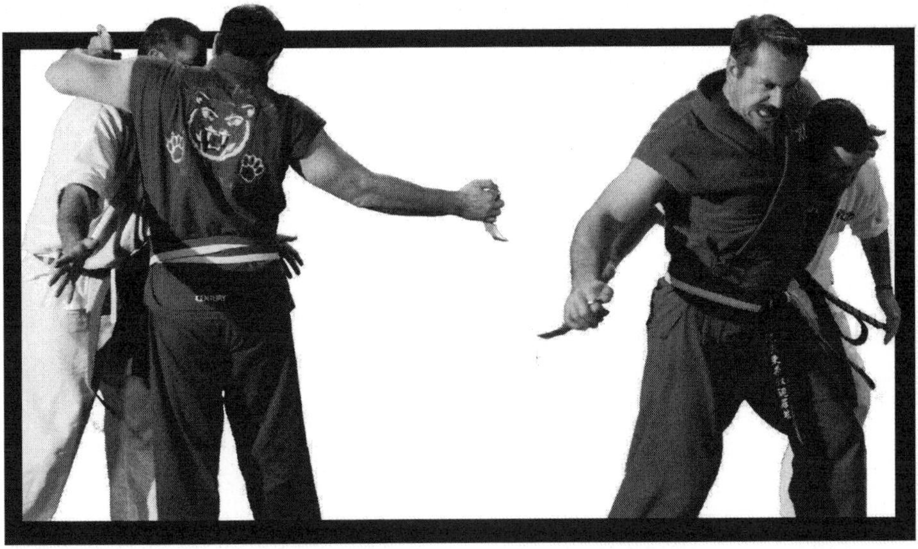

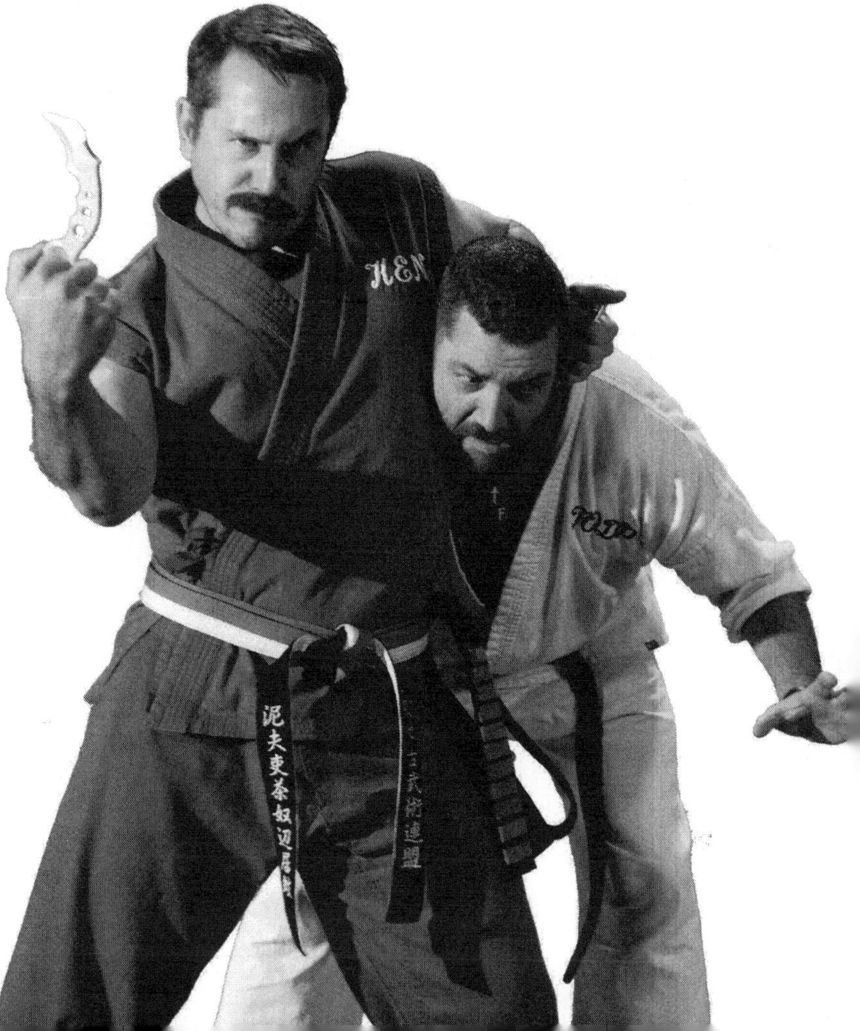
KEN

Insert the blade deep in his ear, piercing the brain and causing massive internal bleeding (destroying the brain) while stabbing into the subclavian artery on the other side of the neck...

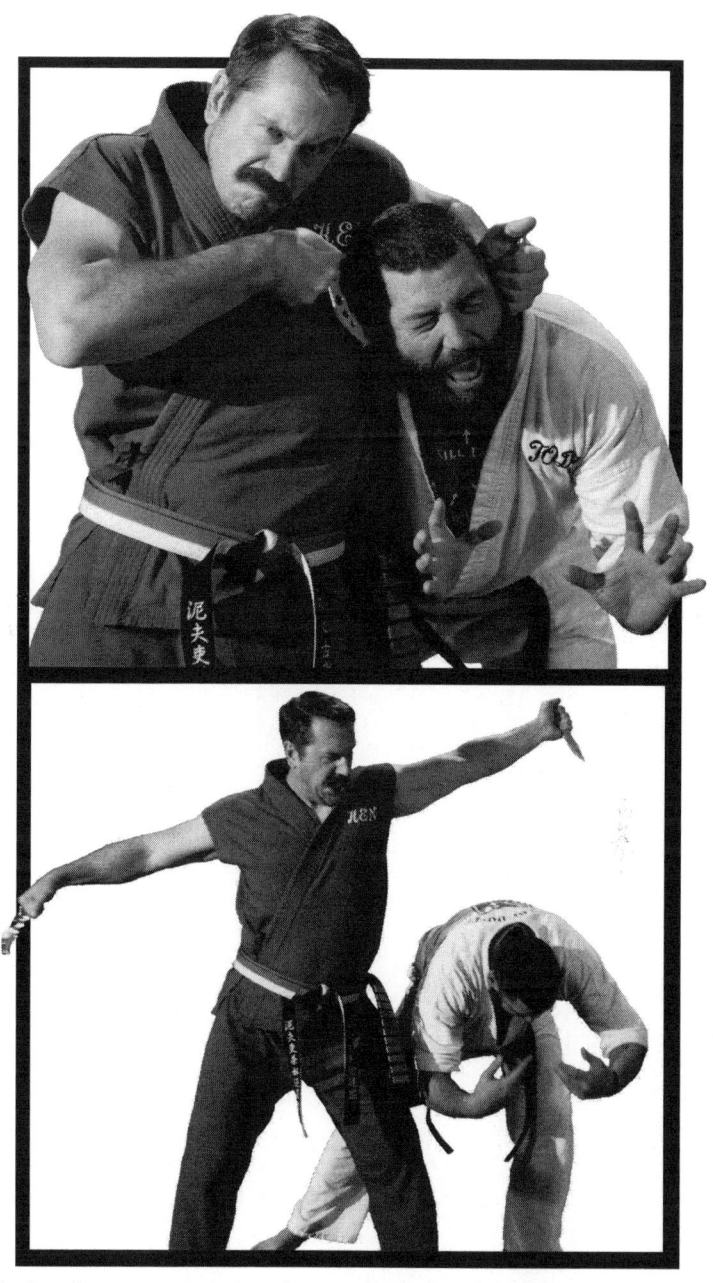

Then pull the knives out and watch him fall like a sack of brain-dead potatoes.

NINJUTSU IS BULLSHIT

REASON #1

They Wear Masks.

They claim to cover their faces in order to protect their identities. It's more likely that they wear masks out of embarrassment. Most masks are made of a poly/cotton blend. I say that the mask and the art are 20% cotton and 70% bullshit.**

REASON #2

Too Many Weapons.

The Ninja are far too dependent on a variety of weapons including swords, throwing stars and poison darts (none of which will make it through an airport metal detector). What if they get attacked on an airplane or in the shower or on an airplane while showering?

Thanks to Ameri-Do-Te my Tiger Claw is always with me. Even when I'm naked I'm still fully armed.

** The remaining 10% is made of unidentified material although judging from the smell I'd have a guess.

REASON #3

They Only Fight At Night.

Being trained for combat under the cover of night might prepare you for battling glitter-covered vampires or deranged insomniacs but life and death confrontations can happen at any time. That's why Ameri-Do-Te is open for business 24/7.**

REASON #4

They Wear Pajamas.

Just like the laziest friend of yours that wears the same mustard-stained tracksuit everyday, I've only ever seen the Ninja dressed in form-fitting black pajamas. And I'm sure that they are the most dangerous girls at the slumber party. But in Ameri-Do-Te we don't have slumber parties. We have slaughter parties. Who's on the guest list? Violent offenders. With serial rapists as their plus one.***

**Technically classes are held from 6:30pm to 8pm Monday through Thursday.

The word "party" here is used as a metaphor for a street fight. I don't throw parties for violent offenders or rapists. But I will happily introduce them to my favorite club.*

****Technically my club is a hammer.

REASON #5

They Have No Fight Record.

Some people say I'm being too hard on the Ninja. And it's true that I've never actually witnessed any student of Ninjutsu in a real street fight. I've also never seen a unicorn eating a candy apple.

That's because neither of those things have ever happened.

Photo by Cheri Frost

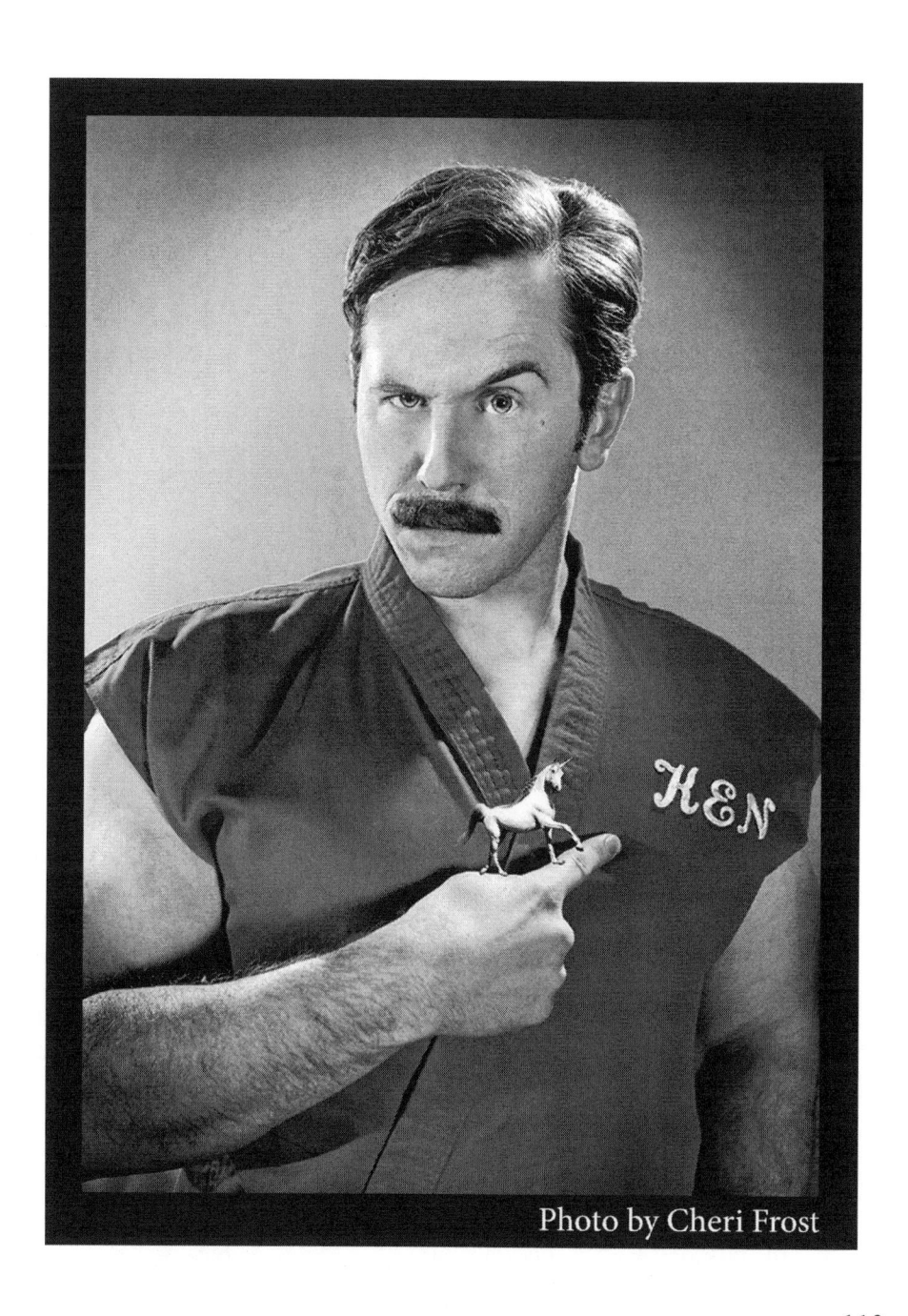

SELFIE DEFENSE

Technology can be a blessing and a curse. Seems like every time I see someone walking through a parking lot nowadays they're looking at their phones. Everybody has their Goo Goo Glasses and their Dick Tracy watches and they're texting while driving and Facebooking while Fapping and Snacking while Snatchchatting. Meanwhile they're not seeing threats in the world around them.

Since this is a generational issue I've invited Katyia here to help me with the demonstration. Katyia is what is known as a "Millennial"**.

** "Millennial" is Latin for "A Breed of Plant that Dies Very Young."

Katyia and I are going to take a "Selfie".

There are two common components:

1) A "Selfie Stick".

2) A "Duck Face".

One of the most dangerous threats to a Selfie is the "Photobomber"!

This person will sneak up unnoticed, inserting himself into your photo and your personal space. Who knows what he is after?!

Step One:
Shorten your stick.

This assures the screen will be closer to your face increasing the chances of you spotting a potential threat.

Step Two: Relax your face. The Duck Face draws blood away from the eyes impairing your vision.

I recommend loosening your face by shaking your head from side to side.

I call this: "Motorboating".

This time when the dreaded "Photo-bomber" returns we are ready!

We see his approach on the screen of our phone...

...and turn our "Selfie Stick" into a weapon!

121

After delivering a series of strikes in close range, wrap your hands around that Selfie Stick with your best golfing grip.

Line up your putt.

Keep your eye on the ball.

Remember to yell "Fore"!**

**There is a slight chance that this technique will cause you to temporarily lose your phone. We call it a "Hole in One."

If this happens just follow your attacker around until his next bowel movement. Don't forget to wear rubber gloves.

123

WAR OF THE WORDS

Ameri-Do-Te is such a revolutionary self defense system that it has caused quite a lot of controversy in the world of traditional martial arts.

You could say that I've made more waves than Steven Seagal sitting on a Russian prostitute's waterbed.

Here are screenshots of some feedback I've received online.

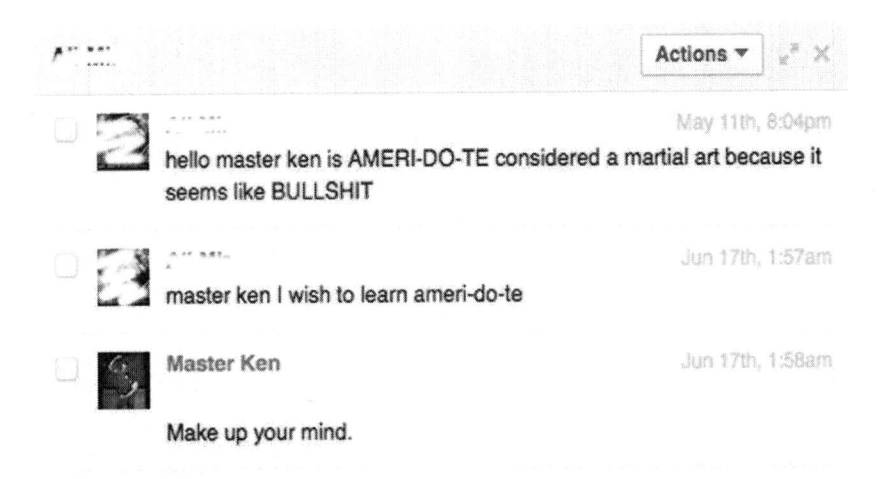

> May 11th, 8:04pm
> hello master ken is AMERI-DO-TE considered a martial art because it seems like BULLSHIT

> Jun 17th, 1:57am
> master ken I wish to learn ameri-do-te

> **Master Ken** — Jun 17th, 1:58am
> Make up your mind.

ALL COMMENTS (99)

Add a public comment...

Top comments ▼

e   6 hours ago (edited) · LINKED COMMENT
This one wasn't funny. It was like: "Hey, why Mr. Ken is so rude and why are his students so wrong?". Just read the contract and do the things right way. Other series Mr/Master Ken was funny, not this time really. Too bad. I wasted 6 min. 13 sec. + had to write the comment not happy for this as I am. Please, hire an odder script diter. Seriously.

Reply

ALL COMMENTS (1,088)

Add a public comment...

Top comments ▼

c   d go   1 day ago · LINKED COMMENT
a dirt too tiny but if the dirt get in your eyes you cry like a monkey hahahahahahaha,and don't think your a big monkey if a tiny dirt get in your eyes you cry like a baby monkey hahahahahahahaah KEN MARTIAL ART BULLSHIT

Reply

T.   n ▶ Master Ken
4 hrs ·

Lost another follower talking sh t about jujitsu watch any of us snap you like a twig

1 Like

👍 Like   💬 Comment   ➔ Share

Master Ken likes this.   Chronological ▾

125

> F**: you're the man

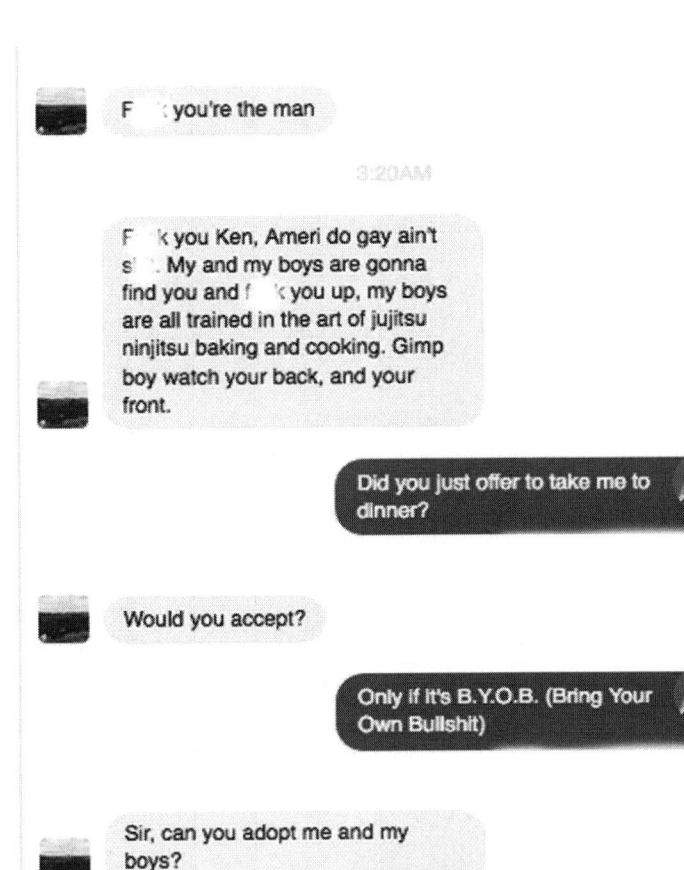

3:20AM

> F**k you Ken, Ameri do gay ain't s***. My and my boys are gonna find you and f**k you up, my boys are all trained in the art of jujitsu ninjitsu baking and cooking. Gimp boy watch your back, and your front.

Did you just offer to take me to dinner?

> Would you accept?

Only if it's B.Y.O.B. (Bring Your Own Bullshit)

> Sir, can you adopt me and my boys?

Shoot me a headcount and I'll check with the fire marshal.

You need to quit posing as a black belt you suck

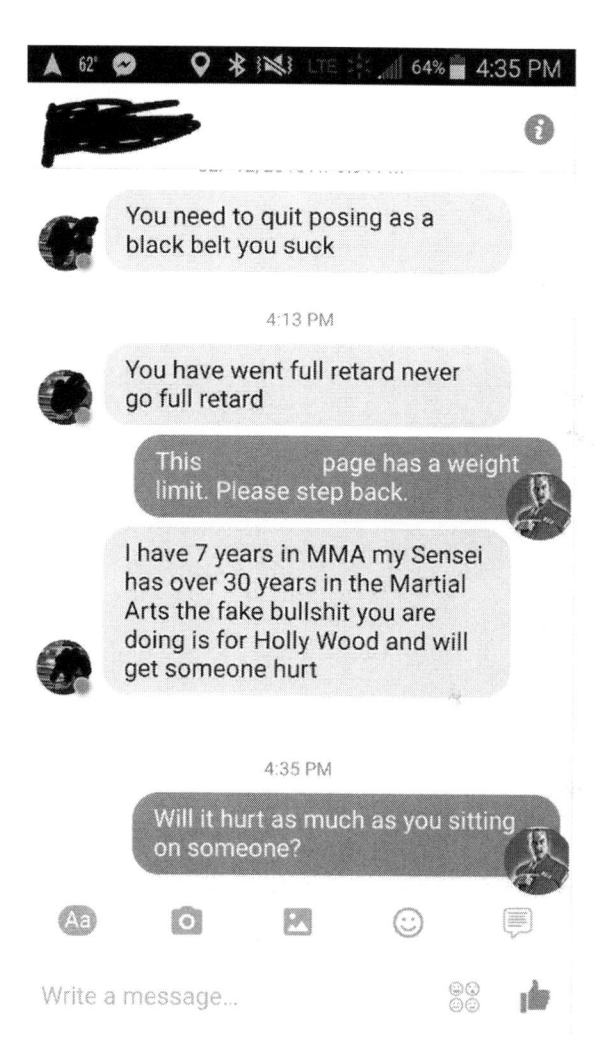

4:13 PM

You have went full retard never go full retard

This ▇▇▇▇▇ page has a weight limit. Please step back.

I have 7 years in MMA my Sensei has over 30 years in the Martial Arts the fake bullshit you are doing is for Holly Wood and will get someone hurt

4:35 PM

Will it hurt as much as you sitting on someone?

Master Ken was mentioned in a post.

[img] ~~Pat Nolan~~ ▸ **Epilepsy Foundation**
12 mins · 🌐

Master Ken thinks epilepsy is a joke. This was his response when I told him his seizure related joke wasn't funny

Let him know what you think

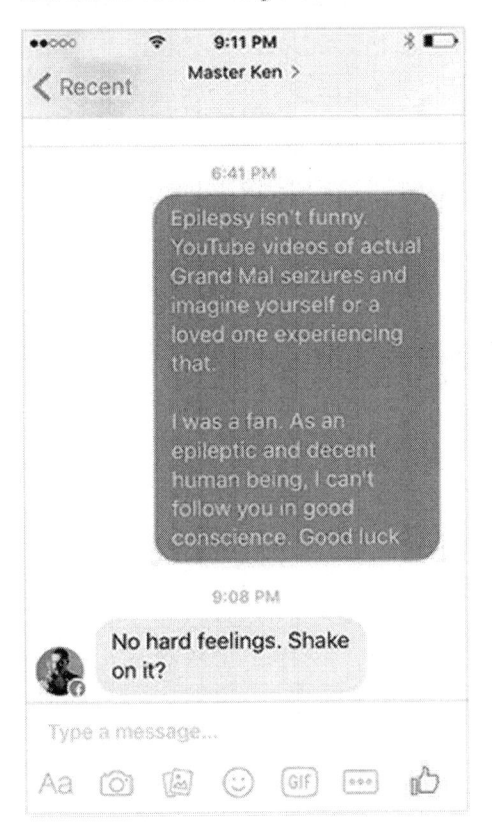

> **Master Ken**
>
> 6:41 PM
>
> Epilepsy isn't funny. YouTube videos of actual Grand Mal seizures and imagine yourself or a loved one experiencing that.
>
> I was a fan. As an epileptic and decent human being, I can't follow you in good conscience. Good luck
>
> 9:08 PM
>
> No hard feelings. Shake on it?

My publisher says I'm a few pages short and that if I don't add a few more then the book will be printed without a "spine"... whatever that means.

I said that was unacceptable. Can't let people go around saying that Ameri-Do-Te is spineless. So... just filling space here.

You know what else is bullshit? Tai Chi.

A martial art designed specifically for kids and old people.

No practical application whatsoever.

I once saw a Tai Chi instructor get beat up by a *mime*.

Choked him with an imaginary rope and then threw him into an invisible wall.

Say, have you ever been on the cover of Black Belt Magazine?

No? I have. Just thought I'd point that out. Here's proof:

SPECIAL ISSUE: 2014 BLACK BELT HALL OF FAME WINNERS

BLACK BELT

WORLD'S LEADING MAGAZINE OF MARTIAL ARTS

Meet the Man Behind YouTube Sensation

MASTER KEN

Founder of Ameri-Do-Te

EXCLUSIVE: MAXIMIZE YOUR PUNCHING POWER NOW!

INVESTIGATIVE REPORT

HOW GOOD CAN YOU GET WITH A SWORD IN 3 DAYS?

COMBAT SPORTS IN JAPAN
Past and Present

Proven Program for BUILDING CORE STRENGTH

PAUL VUNAK
Master Your Emotions in the Dojo

DEC. 2014/JAN. 2015 Display until 1/27/15
$5.99 US $6.99 CAN
blackbeltmag.com

"KILL FACE"
a.k.a.
The Deadliest Technique of All

If you've made it this far and learned all of the techniques in this book then I know you're serious about Ameri-Do-Te. That's why I left the deadliest chapter for last.

Having a good Kill Face is like walking around with a loaded gun in your pocket. Only it's not in your pocket. *It's in your face.*

For liability purposes I must state that I am not responsible for anyone who is injured or killed by looking at the final technique in this book.

Proceed at your own risk!

Okay. Here we go.

3...

2...

1...

KILL FACE!

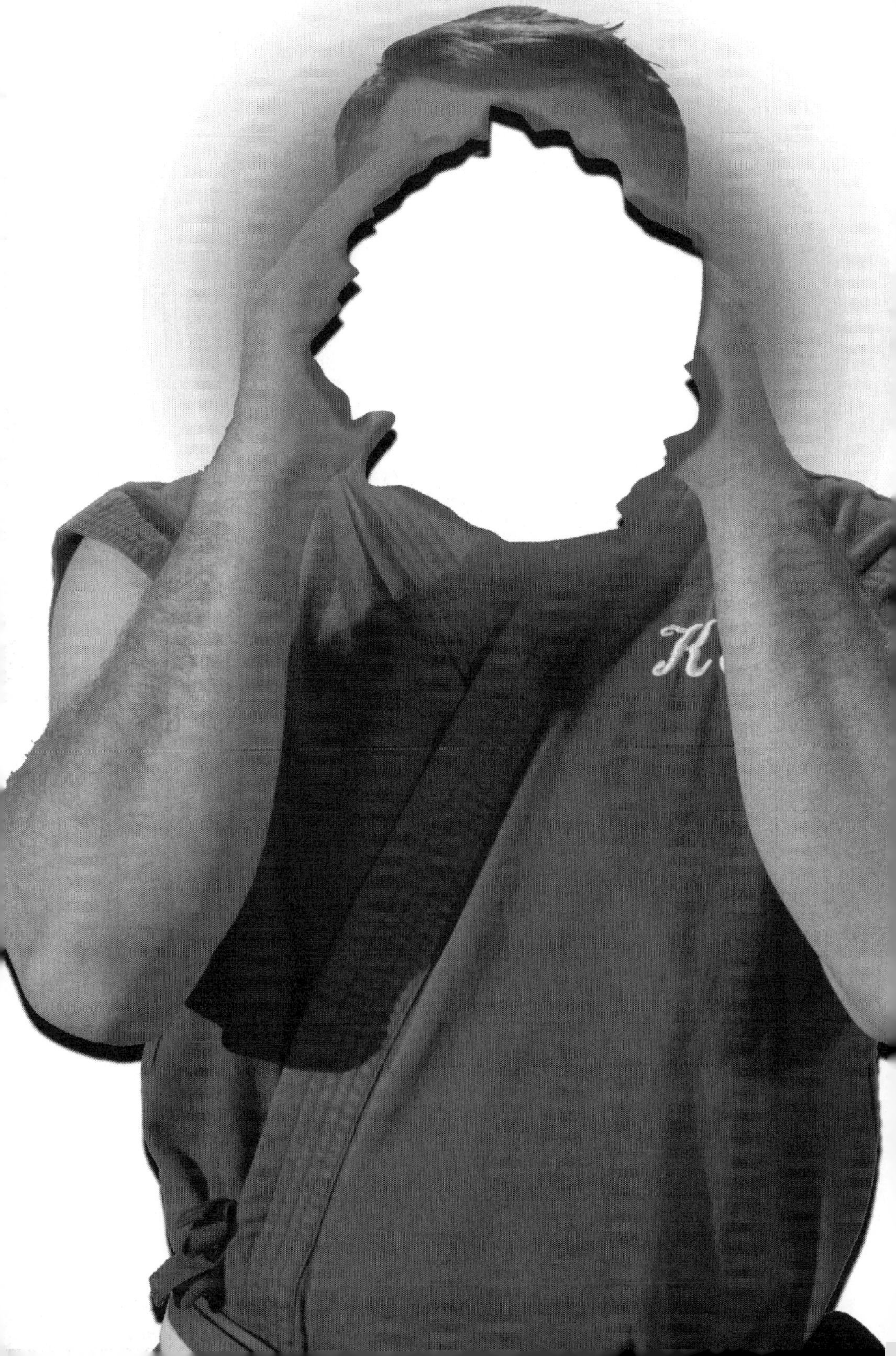

RAINMAKER
MEMBERSHIP SYSTEMS

THESE 8 SIMPLE WORDS GET NEW STUDENTS IN JUST HOURS...

Want the 8 word email Tom used to enroll 15 new students into his martial arts school in less than 7 hrs, WITHOUT using flyers, door hangers, ad cards and all those other ineffective things that take up lots of time with low returns?

Go here → **FreeMagicEmail.com**

Stop wasting your time and money on "old fashioned" marketing. The simple 8 word email script will get you a flood of responses within hours, virtually guaranteed ...

Having had my own school for 20+ years, and spending thousands of dollars and hours on marketing that just didn't work, I discovered a simple email (that is only 8 words long) you can send to your prospective students and get a flood of responses. Get this proven email now so you can copy and paste it and get at least 3 new trials by the end of the day.

Start getting more trials now!
Go here → **FreeMagicEmail.com**

Scott Dolloff
Founder and CEO

ANYTHING ELSE IS CHILD'S PLAY.

CenturyMartialArts.com • (800) 626-2787

CENTURY.
World Leader in Martial Arts Since 1976

"Century" is a registered trademark of Century, LLC. All rights reserved. © 2018 Century, LLC.

BLACK BELT MEMORY
黒帯の記憶

READ THIS IF YOU ARE
TIRED OF FORGETTING EVERYTHING
EARN YOUR BLACK BELT IN MEMORY IN ONLY 21 DAYS

LEARN TO REMEMBER

- ✓ **Names**
- ✓ **Decks of Cards**
- ✓ **Master Ken's jokes**
- ✓ **Numbers**
- ✓ **Facts**
- ✓ **Details**
- ✓ **What you read and everything else.**

Taught by 2x USA Memory Champion, Ron White.

Download free memory tricks book at unmymemory.com

Printed in Great
Britain
by Amazon